Russian Military Forecasting Translation Volume

1999–2018

CLINT REACH

Prepared for the Russia Strategic Initiative,
United States European Command

NATIONAL DEFENSE RESEARCH INSTITUTE

For more information on this publication, visit www.rand.org/t/RRA198-5

Library of Congress Cataloging-in-Publication Data is available for this publication.
ISBN: 978-1-9774-0683-5

Published by the RAND Corporation, Santa Monica, Calif.
© Copyright 2022 RAND Corporation
RAND® is a registered trademark.

Support RAND
Make a tax-deductible charitable contribution at
www.rand.org/giving/contribute

www.rand.org

Preface

This translation volume compiles texts by Russian military experts and covers key factors in Russian military forecasting. These factors include the military-political situation and the military potential of global leaders, such as the United States, China, Russia, Germany, and Japan, among others. Russian strategic deterrence potential is a mitigating factor to threats resulting from hostile intentions of a militarily superior opponent. Translations were produced with permission from East View Information Services and Moscow State University Press.

The research reported here was completed in October 2020 and underwent security review with the sponsor and the Defense Office of Prepublication and Security Review before public release.

This publication was sponsored by the Russia Strategic Initiative, United States European Command, and conducted within the International Security and Defense Policy Center of the RAND National Security Research Division (NSRD), which operates the National Defense Research Institute (NDRI), a federally funded research and development center sponsored by the Office of the Secretary of Defense, the Joint Staff, the Unified Combatant Commands, the Navy, the Marine Corps, the defense agencies, and the defense intelligence enterprise.

For more information on the RAND International Security and Defense Policy Center, see www.rand.org/nsrd/isdp or contact the director (contact information provided on the webpage).

Contents

Figures

Tables

Summary

This report is a translation volume of collected articles on military forecasting from Russian-language sources. It serves as a case study in how Russia conducts forecasting to inform strategic planning. The critical factors include the expected trajectory of the military-political situation, the combined military potential of both Russia and its possible allies and adversaries, and the ability of Russia's strategic deterrence potential to mitigate military threats. This volume shows how Russian military scientists consider these factors in the forecasting process, the objective of which is to build a military that possesses enough conventional and nuclear combat potential to ensure that Russia cannot be intimidated by a stronger adversary or lose a future war.

Editing and Translation Note

Figures and tables are not numbered as they were in the articles in which they originally occurred. They have been renumbered for reader ease.

The italicized paragraphs at the beginning of each chapter are summaries provided by the editor/translator. These were not part of the original content. Brackets indicate content added by the author.

Translations were produced with permission from East View Information Services and Moscow State University Press.

Editor's Note

Russian military writing often contains complex, technical terms or terms of art that might not have clear English counterparts. In such cases, the editor inserted the transliterated Russian in brackets using the Library of Congress transliteration system.[1] Many of these "trouble terms" are compiled in the following list, along with their most common English translations from Russian military texts. As in any language, context is the ultimate determinant of the most appropriate translation. Other notes in English that appear in brackets, including the summaries that precede the articles, are intended to add clarity for the reader. In many cases, figures and tables that were difficult to reproduce in translation were also simplified. Notes in brackets within the translation portion of the volume make the reader aware of these external changes.

aprobirovany	certified
drugye voiska	National Guard, other internal security forces
informatsionnoe protivoborstvo	information confrontation
konfliktnost' obstanovki	level of hostility of a situation, probability of hostile action

---

[1] Library of Congress of the United States, "Russian Romanization Table," webpage, undated.

napravlennaia ugroza	specific threat
napravlennaia voennaia ugroza	specific military threat
nuachnye roty	science companies
nivelirovan	neutralized, mitigated
osnovopolagaiushchiie ustavnye dokumenty	fundamental regulations
provokatsionnye	provocative
sderzhivanie	deterrence
sistema vzgliadov	conceptual system
soedinenie	division or brigade
sub"ekt VPO	VPO actor
teatr voennykh deistvii	theater of military operations
ustrashnenie	intimidation
vnezapnaia proverka	snap (surprise) inspection
voennaia moshch'	military power
voennaia organizatsiia	military organization
voenno-politicheskaia obstanovka (VPO)	military-political situation, a condition of interstate relations characterized by likelihood and character of military conflict

Abbreviations

BRICS   Brazil, Russia, India, China, South Africa

C2   command and control

CSTO   Collective Security Treaty Organization

FSB   Federal Security Service

GDP   gross domestic product

MChS   Ministry of Emergency Situations

MGIMO   Moscow State Institute for International Relations

MGTU   Bauman Moscow State Technical University

MVD   Ministry of Internal Affairs

NATO   North Atlantic Treaty Organization

NDMC   National Defense Management Center

NSS   National Security Strategy

NS   national security

R&D   research and development

SCO   Shanghai Cooperation Organization

TsNII MO   Central Scientific Research Institute of the Ministry of Defense

TVD	theater of military operations
USSR	Union of Soviet Socialist Republics (Soviet Union)
VPO	military-political situation

CHAPTER ONE

Introduction

This volume offers a case study in how the Russian military science community conducts and applies forecasting to inform military planning. The RAND Corporation examined materials from 1999 through 2018 to understand some of the key inputs that the Russian military uses in its planning process. In the works that have been translated in this volume, the international and military-political situation forecasts are important for providing geopolitical scenarios and projected state actions across domains that have direct implications for military requirements.[1] What Russian military planners seek to achieve through forecasting is clarity on the potential hostile intentions of a state actor or coalition, the aggregate military power of that potential adversary, and the necessary force structure of the Russian military organization to mitigate future threats.

Background

Two formative international crises in 2011 convinced senior Russian leadership that the character of modern war was evolving: the Arab Spring and Western military intervention in Libya. The primary lesson

---

[1] See, for example, V. S. Voloshko and V. I. Lutovinov, *Voennaia politika i voennaia bezopasnost' Rossiiskoi Federatsii v usloviiakh globalizatsii*, Moscow: Voennoe izdatel'stvo, 2007; A. A. Dynkin, ed., *Mir 2035. Global'nyi prognoz*, Magistr, 2017; and V. M. Burenok, ed., *Kontseptsiia obosnovaniia perspektivnogo oblika silovykh komponentov voennoi organizatsii Rossiiskoi Federatsii*, Izdatel'skii dom Granitsa, 2018.

that Russian leaders took from these events is that modern war involves the *external* fomenting of a local population to rise against a ruling regime, diplomatic and economic measures to weaken the state, and possibly the application of military force.[2] In Russia, large protests against the results of the 2011 parliamentary elections and against the return of Vladimir Putin to the presidency consolidated such views in the Kremlin and served as final catalysts to reconsider the tools of the state that could be used to prevent an Arab Spring or color revolution from emerging at home.[3]

Russian leadership believed that, at the time, a change in the military-political situation (*voenno-politicheskaia obstanovka*, or VPO, in Russian) had occurred, and this led to administrative reforms and updated guidance documents for military planning.[4] In 2013, Putin signed a decree that broadened the authority of the General Staff to forecast possible domestic unrest supported from abroad as well as oversee military and internal security responses to that contingency. The expanded authority of the General Staff was focused as much on the internal nonmilitary threats as the external military threats. Some of the details of the Statute on the General Staff, or *Polozhenie o general'nom shtabe*, in the "On Defense" law, were outlined by Gera-

---

[2] Vladimir Mukhin, "Moskva korektiruet Voennuyu doktrinu," *Nezavisimaya gazeta*, August 1, 2014. The threat of *noncontact warfare* (the employment of conventional long-range precision munitions against military, political, and military-economic infrastructure) would likely characterize the use of force.

[3] From Russia's perspective, a *color revolution* is a forceful shift in the political status quo—instigated or supported from abroad—whose outcome is unfavorable to Russian interests. The 2003 Rose Revolution in Georgia and the 2004 Orange Revolution in Ukraine are common examples.

[4] The U.S. term that most closely resembles the Russian VPO is *strategic environment* as it is described in the 2018 National Defense Strategy (Jim Mattis, *Summary of the 2018 National Defense Strategy of the United States of America: Sharpening the American Military's Competitive Edge*, Washington, D.C.: U.S. Department of Defense, 2018).

simov in two speeches to the Academy of Military Sciences in 2014 and 2015.[5]

The new authorities of the General Staff included the mandate to coordinate operational and mobilization training activities not only of the armed forces but of "other forces," such as the National Guard, the Federal Security Service (FSB), the Ministry of Emergency Situations (MChS), and special formations created in wartime from the Ministries of Health, Transportation, and Economic Development, among others.[6] These legislative changes also led to a requirement to reexamine the structure of Russia's *military organization (voennaia organizatsiia)*, a term that relates to the armed forces and the other entities mentioned previously that have a role in the event of a military crisis.[7]

These details and above geopolitical context were discussed by the Chief of the Russian General Staff, Valerii Gerasimov, in a 2014 speech before the Academy of Military Sciences. Gerasimov stated that the General Staff was creating a new guidance document that would specify the "primary principles of state policy in the area of military force structure and a conceptual system [*sistema vzgliadov*] detailing the objectives, tasks, directions, and activities for structuring and developing the military organization of the Russian Federation. . . ."[8] This statement was important for military forecasting because it raises a question: How does Russia conceptualize and plan for structuring and developing the military organization of the Russian Federation? The official outcome of the conceptual system that was under development at that time remains unknown. However, available information indicates how some in the Russian military science community frame

---

[5]   V. V. Gerasimov, "Rol' General'nogo shtabe v organizatsii oborony strany v sootvetstvii s novym polozheniem o General'nom shtabe, utverzhdennym prezidenta Rossiiskoi Federatsii," *Vestnik Akademii voennykh nauk*, Vol. 1, No. 46, 2014; and V. V. Gerasimov, "Opyt strategicheskogo rukovodstva v Velikoi otechestvennoi voyni i organizatsiia edinogo upravleniia oboronoi strany v sovremennykh usloviiakh," *Vestnik Akademii voennykh nauk*, Vol. 2, No. 51, 2015.

[6]   Gerasimov, 2014, p. 17. Russia created the National Guard in 2016. Prior to this, internal security troops were subordinate to the Ministry of Internal Affairs.

[7]   Gerasimov, 2014, p. 17.

[8]   Gerasimov, 2014, p. 16.

the problem of justifying force structure and development of the military organization.

In 2014, experts from the 46th Central Scientific Research Institute of the Ministry of Defense (46th TsNII MO), whose primary focus is support of development of the State Armaments Program and the defense-industrial base, were coordinating joint research with civilian institutions such as the Bauman Moscow State Technical University (MGTU), the Moscow State Institute for International Relations (MGIMO), the Institute of the United States and Canada, and the research organizations of the Ministry of Economic Development and the Russian Academy of Sciences. The experts developed international scenarios and military threat forecasts through the year 2035.[9] The methodology used in this research was partially explained in a 2014 *Military Thought* article by the lead investigator, General-Major (ret.) Sambu Tsyrendorzhiev, a senior researcher at the 46th TsNII. Between 2014 and 2018, this work was expanded to incorporate other researchers with expertise in strategic deterrence and military economics. The result was the publication of a book entitled *A Framework for the Justification of the Future Structure of the Force Components of the Military Organization of the Russian Federation* (*Kontseptsiia obosnovaniia perspektivnogo oblika silovykh komponentov voennoi organizatsii Rossiiskoi Federatsii*).[10]

The methodological approach caught the attention of Sergei Belokon', who, as of 2018, was the head of the analytic research department of the Main Operations Directorate of the General Staff. Writing in the *Bulletin of Moscow State University*, Belokon' explained that at that time, there was not a consolidated approach to connect future VPOs with force structure and training.[11] Instead, a patchwork of loosely related methods and models were used to make several assessments and forecasts related to military planning decisions on force structure

---

[9]   S. R. Tsyrendorzhiev, "O kolichestvennoi otsenke stepeni voennoi bezopasnosti," *Voennaia mysl'*, No. 10, 2014, pp. 30–31; and Sambu Tsyrendorzhiev, "Prognoz voennykh opasnostei i ugroz Rossii," *Zashchita i bezopasnost'*, Vol. 4, 2015.

[10]   Burenok, 2018.

[11]   Belokon', 2018, p. 30.

and training of the armed forces and other forces, such as the National Guard. Belokon' argued that the approach developed within the 46th TsNII was preferable because it consolidated a variety of methods into a single assessment tool that could produce indicators that military leadership could use to inform their recommendations to political decisionmakers.[12] Thus, by examining the methodology in the 2014 article (and in the aforementioned 2018 book), it is possible to understand some of the key inputs that the Russian military uses, however independently, to conduct planning through forecasting.

Selection Process and Organization

The selection process for these articles began with the 2018 piece by Sergei Belokon' that highlighted the 46th TsNII's methodology. Given Belokon's position, his endorsement suggested delving more deeply into the methodology. Research for this volume found that there was a connection between the work of the 46th TsNII and the requirement for a conceptual system to justify the structure and development of the Russian military organization, which was mentioned by Gerasimov in his 2014 speech.[13] The methodology provides a useful framework to analyze Russian military assessments and forecasts. For example, the identification within Russian military literature of comparisons of *military potential*—a measure encompassing economic, political, and armed forces potential—can show how Russia measures itself against other powers, such as the United States and China. This could have a number of implications for military planning and strategy as well as on Russian willingness to preemptively use force. Furthermore, the 2015 article by Tsyrendorzhiev (translated in this volume) presents Russian thinking on the character, probability, and source of military threats. In brief, this information is critical to follow the Russian military planning process and the rationale for force structure recommendations and training activities.

---

[12] Belokon', 2018, p. 30.

[13] Burenok, 2018, p. 16.

The volume is organized chronologically with the exception of the 2014 speech by Gerasimov. This translation is presented first because it provides the context for the subsequent content. The 1999 piece on the VPO by V. M. Barynkin follows to familiarize the concepts discussed in the subsequent translations. There is not perfect alignment in Russian military literature about how the VPO is assessed and forecasted since 1999, but the inputs for conducting threat assessments are consistent across a number of the sources reviewed for this report.[14] VPO inputs include the projected global and regional state actions in the military, economic, social, and political domains that, over time, could create greater tension between states and increase the probability of military conflict.

The two articles by Tsyrendorzhiev offer the most important substance of the volume. They collectively provide a useful overview of the key elements of Russian military forecasting. Moreover, some observers have described the 46th TsNII as the "leading scientific-research institute of the Ministry of Defense," and the overall findings of the threat forecast are generally consistent with other official statements and strategic documents.[15] The final article in the volume by Belokon' offers a bureaucratic perspective, explaining the current Russian legislation and processes for assessing the condition of national security (of which

---

[14] Yu. V. Chuev and Yu. B. Mikhailov, *Prognozirovanie v voennom dele [Forecasting in Military Affairs: A Soviet View]*, trans. DGIS Multilingual Section, Translation Bureau, Secretary of State Department, Ottawa, Canada, Washington, D.C.: Department of the Air Force, February 6, 1981; Tsyrendorzhiev, 2014; A. I. Podberezkin, ed., *Strategicheskoe prognozirovanie i planirovanie vneshnei i oboronnoi politiki*, Moscow: MGIMO University Press, Vol. 1, 2015; I. M. Popov and M. M. Khamzatov, *Voina budushchego*, 3rd ed., Moscow: Kuchkovo pole, 2018; and S. P. Belokon', "Otsenivanie sostoianiia natsional'noi i voennoi bezopasnosti Rossii: ustanovlennyi poriadok i vozmozhnye puti sovershenstvovaniia [The Assessment of the Condition of Russian National and Military Security: Established Process and Possible Paths to Improvement]," *Vestnik Moskovskogo gosudarstvennogo universiteta, Seriia 25, Mezhdunarodnye otnosheniia i mirovaia politika*, Vol. 1, 2018.

[15] E. A. Derbin and A. I. Podberezkin, "Perspektivnyi oblik voennoi organizatsii Rossiiskoi Federatsii," *Vestnik MGIMO Universiteta*, Vol. 3, No. 30, 2018.

military security is a part) and how the methodology of the 46th TsNII might improve the process and results.[16]

Figure 1.1 summarizes the interaction between the overarching concepts for military forecasting that are described in this volume: the level of hostility in the VPO, the comparison of military potential of states, and the influence of Russia's strategic deterrence potential on military threats.[17] There is consistency over several decades in the factors considered in Russian assessments and forecasts related to force structure requirements.[18]

Original Russian Authors

The original authors of the works translated in this volume are listed in Table 1.1.

Editing and Translation Note

Figures and tables are not numbered as they were in the articles in which they originally occurred. They have been renumbered for reader ease.

---

[16] A critical question that this volume does not address is which financial considerations are involved in military force structure. The Russian military can have a highly sophisticated approach to developing requirements for the force structure of its military organization, but the corresponding resources to execute fulfillment are ultimately decided by the political leadership. These political decisions, in addition to recommendations from the Minister of Defense, are also informed by forecasts conducted by the Ministry of Economic Development and the Ministry of Finance. Nevertheless, an understanding of military forecasting and its role in the military planning process remains a critical element in Russian decisionmaking.

[17] See also Table 5.4 of this volume.

[18] See, for example, Chuev and Mikhailov, 1981; Podberezkin, 2015; Popov and Khamzatov, 2018; and Aleksandr Pozdniakov, "Metodologiia otsenki voenno-politicheskoi obstanovki v interesakh obespecheniia gosudarstvennoi bezopasnosti Rossiiskoi Federatsii," lecture for the FSB, undated.

Figure 1.1
Framework for Assessing and Forecasting the Level of Russian Military Security

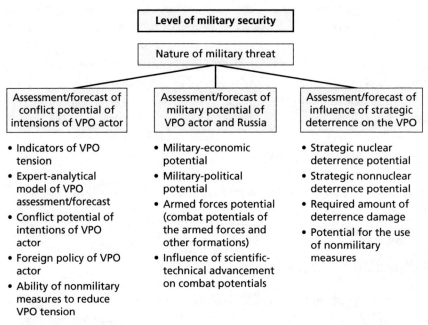

SOURCE: Burenok, 2018, pp. 78–79; Belokon', 2018, p. 30.
NOTE: This figure is an abridged and adapted version of the frameworks from previously mentioned sources.

The italicized paragraphs at the beginning of each chapter are summaries provided by the editor/translator. These were not part of the original content. Brackets indicate content added by the author.

Translations were produced with permission from East View Information Services and Moscow State University Press.

Table 1.1
Original Russian Authors of Translated Works

Name	Rank	Position/Affiliation
V. V. Gerasimov	General	Chief of the Russian General Staff since November 2012
V. M. Barynkin	General-Colonel (Ret.)	Chief of the Main Operations Directorate of the Russian General Staff (1992–1996)
S. R. Tsyrendorzhiev	General-Major (Ret.)	Senior researcher at the 46th TsNII MOD
S. P. Belokon'	Doctor of technical sciences	Head of the Expert-Analytic Department of the Main Operations Directorate of the General Staff (as of 2018)

CHAPTER TWO

The Role of the General Staff in the Organization of Defense of the Country in Accordance with the New Statute on the General Staff, Confirmed by the President of the Russian Federation

The Chief of the Russian General Staff, Valerii Gerasimov, provides an overview of the character of modern warfare and international confrontation as of 2014. These changes, which in part are characterized by increased role of nonmilitary measures to achieve strategic objectives, led to legislative changes that expanded the authorities of the General Staff, which Gerasimov explains in his speech. He calls on the military science community to aid the General Staff in developing a framework for developing the force structure of the military organization of Russia, which includes not only the Armed Forces but internal security forces, among others.[1]

Dear Comrades!

Allow me to welcome the participants of the military-scientific conference of the Academy of Military Sciences.

Over time it has turned out that this event has become focused not only on the summary of the results of the work of the Academy but also on analysis of the activity of military science in general and on determining how to develop and improve it.

In my remarks, I would like to explain the role of the General Staff in the organization of defense of the state and clarify the tasks that are addressed by the military-scientific complex in modern conditions.

---

[1] [Gerasimov, 2014.]

Table 2.1
The Tasks of the General Staff of the Armed Forces of the Russian Federation

The Tasks of the General Staff of the Armed Forces Defined in the Statute on the General Staff, Confirmed by the President of the Russian Federation on July 23, 2013
1. Organization, development, and delivery of the Defense Plan of the Russian Federation for confirmation by the President
2. Coordination of the development of the concepts and plans for the force structure and development of other forces [i.e., internal security troops] and combat formations
3. Monitoring of the condition of the mobilization readiness of other forces, combat formations, and special formations that are stood up in wartime
4. Coordination of the operational and mobilization training of other forces and combat formations
5. Coordination of the development of a command and control [C2] system of other forces, combat formations, and special formations stood up in wartime[;] the determination of the approach of C2 of interagency force groupings[;] and the assurance of centralized combat C2 of those groupings for the purpose of defense
6. C2 of interagency force groupings during the period of direct threat of aggression and in wartime for the purpose of defense, the coordination of the actions of the Armed Forces of the Russian Federation, other forces, and combat formations in peacetime during strategic deterrence activities

In 2013, a new statute on the General Staff was approved by a decree of the President of the Russian Federation.

In general, the nature of the activities of the General Staff did not change. The primary purposes of the General Staff, as before, remain strategic planning in the area of defense, developing the foundation for ensuring the military security of the state, and [establishing] the force structure concepts and development of the Armed Forces and military organization of Russia.

At the same time, according to the new statute, a number of tasks of the General Staff have been clarified, and it has been given additional authorities. Those authorities are directed, first of all, at the coordination of the activities of all federal organs of the executive in the interests of ensuring defense readiness and the security of the country.

Table 2.2
Change in the Character of Armed Conflict

The Use of Political, Diplomatic, Economic, and Other Nonmilitary Measures in Conjunction with the Application of Military Force
• Reduction of the military-economic potential of the state by destroying critically important military and civilian infrastructure
• Simultaneous effects on troops and enemy targets throughout the entire depth of [enemy] territory
• Massed employment of high-precision weapons, the widescale use of special forces troops, and use of robotic systems and weapons based on new physical principles
• Employment of asymmetric and indirect actions
• Armed conflict in all physical domains and the information domain
• C2 of forces and means in a unified information space
• Peacetime forces used at the outset of military actions
• Highly maneuverable noncontact combat actions of joint-force groupings
• Participation of the military-civilian component in combat actions

The expansion of the spectrum of tasks that are conducted by the General Staff is based, above all, on the ongoing changes in the character of armed conflict.

Modern conflicts are fast-paced and are accompanied by the active use of military and nonmilitary means. The makeup of interagency forces that are used for defense is expanding, as is the range of issues of interaction between them and state structures.

Political, diplomatic, economic, and other measures, including those of a discrete nature, such as using international nongovernmental organizations and private military companies, are acquiring greater significance in achieving military-political objectives. Events in Syria and Ukraine are examples, as is the activity of Greenpeace in the Arctic.

The reaction time in the transition from political-diplomatic measures to the employment of military force has reduced exponentially. Decisions on the formation, employment, and support of force groupings are made in real time.

Military actions are drifting into the information and space domains.

The completion of a U.S. global missile defense system, the realization by foreign states of the concept of "Geocentric Theater of Military Operations," "[Prompt] Global Strike," "Network-Centric [Operations]," and the placement of combat-ready forces on a permanent basis in key regions around the world by the leading countries allows these countries to conduct strikes against any point on Earth in a short amount of time.

All of these changes led to the necessity to improve the defense of the Russian Federation [and] to clarify the role of state institutions in the organization of defense and the role of the General Staff. This resulted in the new Statute on the General Staff in the Federal law "On Defense."

One of the new tasks of the General Staff defined in the legislation is the development of the Defense Plan of the Russian Federation. [The Plan] includes a complex of interrelated military planning documents for all of the military organization of the state.

The General Staff, together with the federal executive organs, developed [the] plan, which was confirmed by the President of the Russian Federation in January [2013].

In the course of the development of the plan, the place, time, direction, forces, means, and resources were coordinated for activities related to the timely preparation of the country to transition to wartime conditions and the execution of given tasks by the military organization of the state.

To prevent military conflicts, the comprehensive conduct of whole-of-state strategic deterrence measures has been planned.

The basis of [the strategic deterrence measures] are political-diplomatic and external economic, which are closely tied with military, information, and other measures. In general, [the measures] are intended to convince potential aggressors of the futility of any forms of pressure against the Russian Federation and its allies.

In planning strategic deterrence, the General Staff organized interagency cooperation in the course of executing whole-of-state activities.

Table 2.3
Changes Introduced into the Federal Law "On Defense" from 5 April 2013

Objective of the Changes:	Coordination of Actions of the Organs of State Authority, Military Command, and Local Authorities in the Defense Readiness of the Country
Elevation of the status of the General Staff of the Armed Forces of the Russian Federation (Section 1, Article 2.2)	→ The General Staff of the Armed Forces of the Russian Federation executes the coordination of defense activity within the bounds of its authorities.
Development of the Defense Plan of the Russian Federation (Section 1, Article 2.1)	→ The Defense Plan of the Russian Federation is a complex set of interrelated Russian military planning documents. The development of the documents is conducted in accordance with the Statute on Military Planning in the Russian Federation.
Clarification of the functions of other forces, combat formations, and organs in executing defense tasks (Section 4)	→ Other forces, combat formations, and organs are included in joint operational and mobilization training with the Armed Forces of the Russian Federation to prepare for the execution of defense tasks.
Clarification of the statutes of territorial defense (Section 5)	→ Territorial defense is carried out on the territory of the Russian Federation or in its separate areas where martial law is introduced in coordination with measures taken within the bounds of this legal regime. The sequence of organization, deployment, and execution of territorial defense is defined by the Territorial Defense Plan of the Russian Federation.

The experience of developing the Defense Plan demonstrated the need for clear regulation of joint activity of the federal executive organs.

To this end, the General Staff has prepared a new edition of the Statute on Military Planning in the Russian Federation. This statute defines the process of developing the Defense Plan and creating the list of documents that are a part of the plan, and the organs of state and military command and control that are responsible for developing the accompanying documents.

All of the actions of troops (forces) have been planned in accordance with the fundamental regulations [*osnovopolagaiushchiie ustavnye dokumenty*] of the Armed Forces. These documents were updated and entered into force in 2013. The primary applications of interbranch and coalition troop (force) groupings were defined in these documents, taking into account changes in the character of warfare.

At the same time, there is presently no guidance regulating the employment of interagency force groupings.

Together with the FSB, MVD [Ministry of Internal Affairs], and MChS, the General Staff has begun working on the preparation of such documents.

Another task of the General Staff is the coordination of developing the concepts, plans, force structure, and development of other forces, and combat formations for the purpose of defense.

To this end, a new guidance document is being prepared. In it, the primary principles of state policy in the area of military force structure and a conceptual framework detailing the objectives, tasks, directions, and activities of the force structure and development of the military organization of the Russian Federation will be presented, as well as the conditions for their realization.

In the course of joint activities, exercises, and in the consequence management of emergency situations, such as the floods in the Far East [in 2013], it became clear that the existing C2 systems of federal executive organs participating in defense were not sufficiently linked. This complicates the C2 of troop (force) groupings. [The issue of linkage] is forcing us to take a fresh look at the organization and process of C2 of troop and force groupings consisting of personnel from various agencies. Coordination of the development of the C2 systems of other

Figure 2.1
C2 System of the Military Organization of the Russian Federation

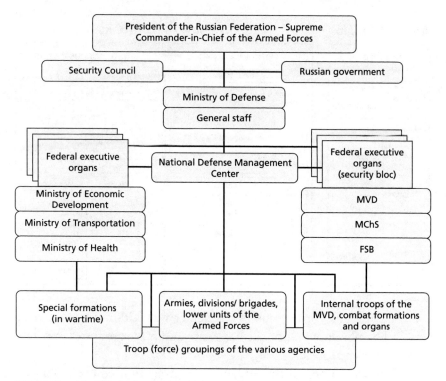

[NOTE: Graphic slightly altered for clarity. No change to content.]

forces, combat formations, and special formations that are created in wartime is required.

To solve these issues, it is necessary to integrate the C2 system of the Armed Forces and of the federal executive organs that are participating in defense into a unified system of state and military C2. At the same time, it is appropriate to maximize the use of the potential of the [existing] infrastructure of these systems and to increase their capabilities.

An important step in the creation of such a C2 system was an initiative by the Minister of Defense to establish the National Defense Management Center [NDMC] of the Russian Federation. On Janu-

Figure 2.2
Forms of Operational Training with the Participation of Federal Executive Organs

Areas of training	Training of C2 organs	
Exercises	**Within C2 organ**	**Within structural units**
Scale: Federal, interregional, regional	**Command training** — Training runs / Command games	**Command training** — Joint / Individual
Objectives: To prepare areas of activity, research (experimental), testing (inspections)	**Small exercises** **Scale:** Federal, interregional, regional / **Organization and methods:** Multiphase, special, joint	**C2 games** **Group small exercises** **Professional training by occupation**
Organization and methods: Multiphase, special, joint	**Objectives:** To prepare areas of activity, research (experimental), testing (inspections) / **Execution:** At everyday locations, alternate C2 locations, computer	**Joint training:** Routine tasks, assembling, games, individual-level training / **Independent training:** Independent work, consultations, execution of tasks, participation in research and historical work

ary 20, 2014, the cornerstone of the center was laid and construction began. The development of the hardware and software systems is happening simultaneously.

With the launch of the NDMC, we have a unified C2 system for the entire military organization of the Russian Federation. This will allow us to obtain and analyze information in real time and to prepare substantiated recommendations for decisions by the state leadership in reaction to crisis situations in the country and abroad.

The execution of defense tasks requires certain knowledge of military affairs from officials of the federal executive organs. Thus, in the Military Academy of the General Staff, we restored joint training of representatives of the ministries and agencies with a course, "National Defense."

To achieve coherence in the work of state organs and military command and control joint-training activities are conducted on a regular basis.

Figure 2.3
The Purpose and Tasks of the Military-Science Complex of the Russian Armed Forces

> **The military-science complex of the Armed Forces of the Russian Federation plays a crucial role in the military organization of the state as the connective tissue between the Armed Forces of the Russian Federation and the Russian scientific community.**

> *The military-science complex is intended for the assurance of the scientific justification of the directions of the force structure and development of the Armed Forces of the Russian Federation and the preliminary scientific work on military-political decisions that are made.*

> The scientific justification of the directions of the force structure and development of the Russian Armed Forces

1. The justification of the primary directions of the force structure and development of the Armed Forces in general, the branches and combat arms of the Russian Armed Forces, and forces that are not part of the branches or combat arms of the Russian Armed Forces.

2. The determination of the optimal correlation of forces and means of the Russian Armed Forces, their qualitative and quantitative composition, and the forms and methods of their employment.

3. The development of the tactical-technical and operational-tactical requirements for future weapons systems and military equipment.

4. The formation and investigation of new scientific trends that have interservice and supra-service implications, taking into consideration the results of forecasting and exploratory research in the interests of the force structure, development, and employment of the Russian Armed Forces in defense of the state.

5. Assurance of the military-scientific and scientific-technical monitoring of ams and equipment throughout their life cycle.

The first experience with such activities was in 2012 during a strategic command-staff training exercise with state organs. [In 2013] during a snap inspection [*vnezapnaia proverka*] ordered by the Supreme Commander-in-Chief that occurred on the sidelines of the strategic exercise Zapad-2013, the interaction between several federal executive organs, the authorities of the subjects of the Russian Federation, and local authorities, was observed and improved.

During joint-training activities, the primary efforts should be focused on improving the organization and joint resolution of tasks by multiagency troop (force) groupings. The activities should be conducted against a general operational-tactical backdrop and based on unified scenarios of the development of the military-political and strategic situation.

Such is the substance of the new tasks defined by the Statute on the General Staff. The execution of these tasks presupposes a large organizational and intellectual effort, which should be carried out methodically and logically. The military-science complex plays an important role in the effort.

Leadership of the military-science complex and the organization of research in the Armed Forces falls on the General Staff.

What are the current tasks that stand before the military-science complex and military science in general?

The most important task is the justification of the primary directions of the force structure and development of the Armed Forces in general, and in the service branches and combat arms [in particular]. The result of the research should be recommendations on the rational composition of the Armed Forces and the optimal correlation of forces and means for armed combat.

Another highly important task is the forecast and assessment of the military threats to the Russian Federation and the development of recommendations based on these findings for improving state defense policy.

It is necessary to identify, at the earliest stage possible, the outbreak and trajectory of possible threats to Russia, and to prepare recommendations to neutralize them with military and nonmilitary methods.

Particular attention should be paid to creating an entire landscape of indirect and asymmetric actions that are carried out by various federal executive organs within a unified plan in the interest of preventative neutralization of threats to the military security of Russia.

Another task of military science is the development of the forms of employing and actions of troop (force) groupings and the determination of their optimal composition.

For this, it is necessary to study the experience of the combat employment of the Armed Forces in conflicts of varying intensity and to identify new military and military-technical trends.

In 2013, a theoretical assessment of possible threats was conducted, ways in which they could form were analyzed, and the capabilities of joint-force groupings in strategic directions (theaters of military operations) were tested.

In general, the obtained results supported the execution of practical tasks.

At the same time, it is necessary to point out that with the increasing role of scientific research, the requirements for the justification of scientific recommendations are also increasing. The spectrum of military-scientific developments is expanding, and forms and methods of research are being improved.

This dynamic is intensifying the need to improve the military-science complex and to bring it into accordance with current and future tasks.

Since 2013, the General Staff has been working on this effort.

With the goal of increasing the effectiveness of scientific work, the roles of the main commands of the service branches and combat arms of the Armed Forces have been strengthened.

The reintroduction of military-scientific units into the military C2 organs has facilitated the organization of direct interaction with the scientific-research institutions.

The scientific-research organizations that were formed in the area of armed conflict ensure that there is comprehensive research into the development of the service branches and combat arms of the Armed Forces and the resolution of issues related to joint interaction of the service branches.

As an experiment, four science companies [*nauchnye roty*] were created.[2] This helped to attract talented graduates from academic institutions to work on solving practical tasks within the Ministry of Defense.

We are currently searching for new ways for the Ministry of Defense to cooperate and coordinate with the military-industrial complex. One example is the Innovation Day of the Ministry of Defense, which took place in August [2012]. Work in this area will continue.

There are other important tasks in the development of the military-science complex for 2014.

First of all, this involves the completion of the formation of the five-year plan for development of the scientific-research organizations of the Ministry of Defense.

The plan is directed at improving structures and building up capability within the military-science complex, the clarification of tasks of the scientific-research organizations, and the modernization of the laboratory-experimental base.

Particular attention should be paid to the training of scientific cadres and the strengthening of the potential of scientific-research organizations. We are looking for new ways to reestablish the prestige and status of the military scientist and are setting up a training system for researchers and developing scientific schools.

We are looking into the formation of a unified system organizing scientific research in the field of defense at the state level. The system will be based on military-theoretical knowledge and the results of fundamental research of the Russian Academy of Sciences, the Academy of Military Sciences, the Russian Academy of Missile and Artillery Sciences, and other scientific organizations, and it will use the potential of military-industrial enterprises.

A significant portion of the scientific developments should be made in the creation of future weapons and military and special equipment.

---

2   [*Companies*, in this case, are small military formations consisting of perhaps a few dozen troops that specialize in computer-related operations.]

We should especially focus on the most relevant high-tech areas. This includes the development of military robotic systems, the creation of future telecommunications infrastructure of the Armed Forces, and the development of strategic deterrence forces and an aerospace defense system.

At the same time, the requirements for future weapon systems must be derived from those methods of armed combat that lead to the most effective counter of forecasted threats to the military security of Russia.

An important area of this work is the formation of a unified base of scientific knowledge. This base will consist of all available and expected results of scientific research and research and development [R&D] projects that have been conducted based on orders of the Ministry of Defense.

Beginning [in 2014], a special collection of reference copies will be created in the military-scientific library of the General Staff. After completion of an integrated, automated accounting [filing] system in 2017, the database will be available to consumers in electronic format.

Table 2.4
Formation of an Integrated Base of Scientific Knowledge

Year	Action
January 2014	Formation of an archive of the results of dissertation research, scientific research, and R&D projects within the Military-Scientific Library of the Armed Forces (the special collection of reference copies is located in Building 3 of the Ministry of Defense of the Russian Federation)
2015	Construction of an automated decisionmaking support system for the organization of scientific work in the Armed Forces of the Russian Federation
2016	Formation of an electronic library of scientific work and an automated accounting system and the storage and analysis of the results of completed R&D and dissertation studies (within the 27th TsNII MOD)
2017	Integration of the information base with similar bases of other federal executive organs (Ministry of Education and Science, Ministry of Industry and Trade of Russia)

We are working to create a specialized center for supporting its formation, buildup, and maintenance.

These are the primary directions in our work to improve the military-science complex.

I would like to emphasize that military science is most effective when the results of scientific work are collected and integrated into practice. All military-scientific studies must be conducted in line with unified military-technical policy that is developed and executed by the General Staff.

In addition to scientific-research organizations and military education institutions of the Ministry of Defense, it is appropriate to more-actively involve the federal executive organs, institutes of the Russian Academy of Sciences, and, of course, the Academy of Military Sciences in research.

The Academy [of Military Sciences] is a basic scientific organization—more professionalism and experience should be brought to the study of ensuring the defense of the Russian Federation.

Particular attention should be focused on the development of a methodology for military force structure and the structure of the Armed Forces and the development of new forms and methods of conducting military actions. The scientific potential of the Academy [of Military Sciences] should be effectively employed in the interest of forming theoretical bases for the conduct of military action and the development of military and nonmilitary measures in modern armed conflicts and assessing the balance between them [military and nonmilitary measures].

In 2014, research in this area and the integration of obtained results into practice should be directed first and foremost at the development of a new Defense Plan of the Russian Federation and the State Armaments Plan for 2016–2025 and toward the execution by the General Staff of its additional authorities in the area of military security and defense of the state.

This joint work should be done within the bounds of research that has already been conducted as well as work that is planned for the near future.

Figure 2.4
Directions for the Joint Work of the Russian Ministry of Defense and the Academy of Military Sciences

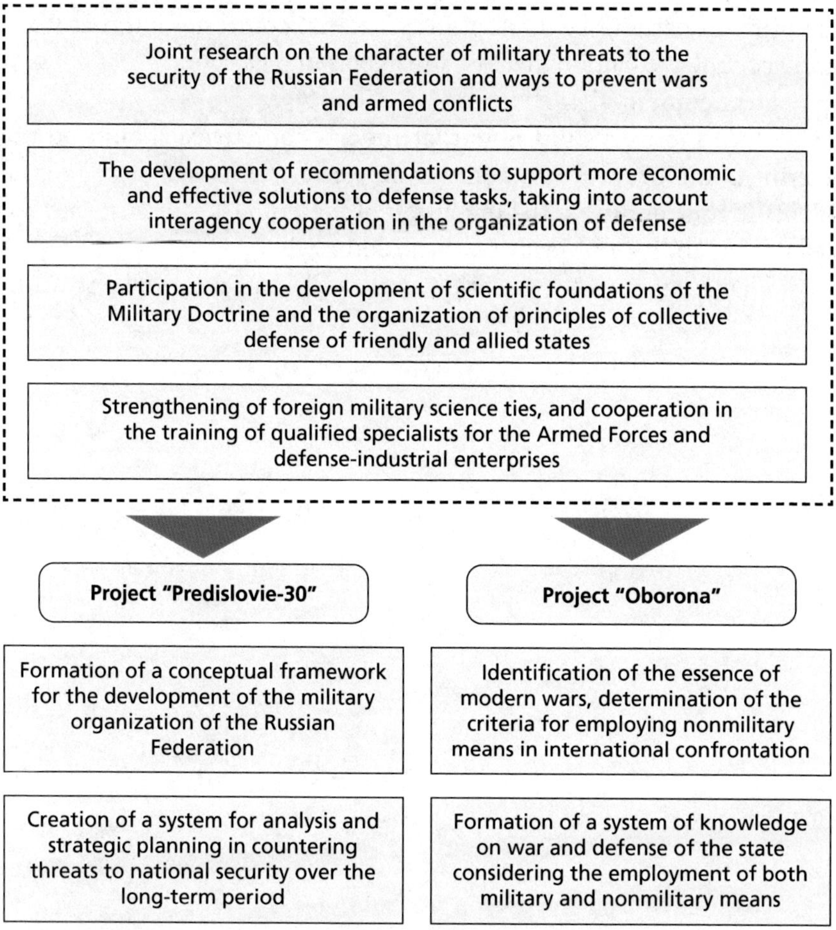

```
┌─────────────────────────────────────────────────────────────────┐
│  ┌─────────────────────────────────────────────────────────┐     │
│  │ Joint research on the character of military threats to the│     │
│  │ security of the Russian Federation and ways to prevent wars│    │
│  │                and armed conflicts                        │     │
│  └─────────────────────────────────────────────────────────┘     │
│  ┌─────────────────────────────────────────────────────────┐     │
│  │ The development of recommendations to support more economic│    │
│  │ and effective solutions to defense tasks, taking into account│   │
│  │ interagency cooperation in the organization of defense     │     │
│  └─────────────────────────────────────────────────────────┘     │
│  ┌─────────────────────────────────────────────────────────┐     │
│  │ Participation in the development of scientific foundations of the│ │
│  │ Military Doctrine and the organization of principles of collective│ │
│  │        defense of friendly and allied states             │     │
│  └─────────────────────────────────────────────────────────┘     │
│  ┌─────────────────────────────────────────────────────────┐     │
│  │ Strengthening of foreign military science ties, and cooperation in│ │
│  │ the training of qualified specialists for the Armed Forces and│   │
│  │          defense-industrial enterprises                  │     │
│  └─────────────────────────────────────────────────────────┘     │
└─────────────────────────────────────────────────────────────────┘
```

Project "Predislovie-30"

Formation of a conceptual framework for the development of the military organization of the Russian Federation	

Project "Oborona"

Identification of the essence of modern wars, determination of the criteria for employing nonmilitary means in international confrontation	

| Creation of a system for analysis and strategic planning in countering threats to national security over the long-term period | Formation of a system of knowledge on war and defense of the state considering the employment of both military and nonmilitary means |

The Academy [of Military Sciences] is already participating in interagency research directed at the determination of the main priorities in the development of the military organization of the Russian Federation over the long-term period under the auspices of the project "Predislovie-30" ["Preface-30"].

Beginning in 2014, on the basis of recommendations from the Academy of Military Sciences, there are plans to begin the project "Oborona" [*Defense*], which is aimed at the creation of a modern knowledge system on war and defense of the state, the identification of the primary patterns of modern international confrontation that takes into account the employment of so-called *soft power*.

Dear comrades!

Once more I would note that today's conference should be the starting point for future cooperation between the General Staff and the scientific community in the resolution of present tasks for ensuring the defense capability and security of the country!

Thank you for your attention and I wish your work to be fruitful.

CHAPTER THREE

Assessment of the Military-Political Situation: Methodological Aspect

The author, Colonel-General Viktor Barynkin, served as the Chief of the Main Operations Directorate of the General Staff from 1992–1996.[1] Barynkin describes the methodology for assessing and forecasting the military-political situation, which is commonly referred to by its Russian acronym, VPO. The VPO is used in Russian military planning to help understand the current and future states of international relations; this understanding is based on such inputs as strategic plans and intentions of possible adversaries, the balance of military power at various levels, the nature of military threats, the likely character of future war, and the probability of war. In American parlance, it roughly could be compared with the strategic environment.

Making timely and appropriate decisions in the area of military policy and military art depends, to a large degree, on the quality of the assessment of the VPO in the world (in this or that region) and its possible changes. The assessment of the VPO and the forecast of its development is, by and large, the prerogative of the senior political and military leadership. However, in the resolution of such tasks, military representatives of the operational-strategic, operational, and operational-tactical levels all participate. Often finding themselves in the center of important political events or conflict situations, these rep-

---

[1] [V. M. Barynkin, "Otsenka voenno-politicheskoi obstanovki: metodologicheskii aspekt," *Voennaia mysl'*, No. 5, 1999, pp. 23–30.]

resentatives must know how to navigate them. Without a clear understanding of the situation, it is not possible to work on military force
structure matters or wisely employ military force for the prevention or
resolution of a conflict. Therefore, officers within the military command staffs must understand the methodology and have practical
skills for assessing the VPO.

Global experience has shown that miscalculations in assessing
the VPO can lead to serious consequences. In particular, this was
confirmed by the events of 1991 in the Persian Gulf. The Americans
warned Kuwaiti leadership on several occasions of the possibility of
Iraqi aggression, including a few days before the invasion of Iraqi forces.
However, Kuwaiti politicians and military members did not agree with
those assessments given by the Americans. "Hussein is bluffing," said
one of the leaders of Kuwait two days before the attack. The result is
well known.

The military-political situation is a historically specific set of conditions and factors connected with the balance of military-political
forces, the nature of the actions of those forces, the condition of relations between those forces, and the use of military force for political
objectives.

The military-political situation is a cross-section of the internal
political situation in the state (or its parts) and the external international situation in some region or in the world in general. Based on the
scale, number of participants, and the breadth of the conditions and
factors that determine the VPO, it is best to categorize it in the following manner: VPO in the world in general; VPO in a separate, large
region—the regional VPO (in an entire continent or a part of it, such
as eastern Europe or the Far East); the VPO in a separate country—the
local VPO; or VPO in a part of a country (in a separate area). Based on
historical conditions, a specific time period, and the nature of relations
between the sides, the VPO can be divided into the peacetime VPO
and wartime VPO.

This is the most general characteristic of the military-political
situation as an object of study. For a complete assessment of the VPO,
it is important to specify its internal composition and structural elements. To do this, it is necessary to highlight those factors (conditions,

circumstances) that make up the specific military-political situation, form the specific type (nature) of military-political relations (allied, friendly, partner, neutral-cautious, tense, confrontational, hostile), and determine the present condition of these factors and the possibilities for change. Those factors are first of all:

- the subjects (sides) of military-political relations: political forces that possess military means and are capable of using them for political objectives
- the geopolitical location of the sides (e.g., territory, borders, neighbors), and the positions and personal qualities of the political leaders and military leadership
- the interests and intentions of the sides, and their objectives, plans, and military doctrines
- military forces of the sides (aggregate military potential, quantity and quality of the armed forces, their composition, condition, lay-down [*dislokatsiia*], and capabilities)
- the military-political actions that the subjects of the VPO take for the achievement of their political objectives (e.g., demonstration of force, the use of force in various forms and at various scales, interposition between warring sides, withdrawal of forces from foreign territories).

Subjects of the VPO can be states and their coalitions, nations, and other social-ethnic groups, classes, parties, or movements. The number of interacting subjects; the composition of those subjects; their condition, scale, geopolitical location, and historical traits; and the nature and direction of their policy all have influence on the VPO. Furthermore, the nature of the ruling elite and its social qualities, positions, tendencies, biases, and its true weight within society and abroad can have a significant impact on the balance of political forces and their manifestation. When extremist forces, adventurous factions, or criminal structures come to power, the situation inevitably worsens and frequently leads to the outbreak of war or armed conflict.

As we know, at the base of any policy lie the interests and objective requirements that form those interests. The latter are determined by the particularities of the historical development of the sides, their geopolitical location, the presence of resources, and other factors. The primary interest of any political force, or class, or nation, or party, or state, is its self-preservation and the assurance of advantageous conditions for its existence and development. In addition, it is typical of a political force to expand its influence, to capture a leading role, to gain new positions, and even to establish economic and political dominance. These two tendencies—self-preservation and the broadening of influence (expansion)—are reflected in the corresponding political and military doctrines, in long-term and short-term objectives, and in concrete plans of action. However, in every case, the sides are compelled to weigh and consider clashing interests.

Not only interests of the state in general but interests of the separate ruling elite, political parties, and national and nationalistic groups can influence the VPO within a country. Sometimes these interests might not coincide with the interests of society or might even stand in direct contradiction to them. Such was the case in Chechnya, Abkhazia-Georgia, Armenia-Azerbaijan, and other conflicts on the territory of the former [Union of Soviet Socialist Republics (Soviet Union, or USSR)].

In regard to the overall VPO in the world, the interests of VPO's primary subjects in some respects align while in others they quite noticeably diverge. For example, the United States is unquestionably interested in maintaining order and stability in the modern world insofar as it has the leading economic, political, and military position. The first part of these interests align with others, while the latter part is a divergence of interests of the United States from the countries of western Europe, Japan, and their policy toward Russia.

Demographic, scientific and technology, and moral-psychological factors, as well as military-economic, information, and military capabilities have significant influence on the nature of military-political relations and on the VPO. In modern conditions, it is not possible to effectively influence the trajectory of the VPO without sufficiently high military and economic potential. But if the economic and military capabilities of the VPO participants to change the VPO are studied well enough, the information resulting from such research could be used in a way that would reduce [the stronger side's ability to affect the situation to its benefit].

The quantitative characteristics of the armed forces naturally influence the VPO. However, today, qualitative and structural elements of the armed forces as well as informational, technical, and moral-psychological superiority of one state over another subjects in military-political relations are acquiring more significance. The combat capabilities of weapons and military equipment, the appearance of new types of each, the personnel training system, changes in the organizational structure of the armed forces, and greater emphasis on offense or defense all have impacts on the nature of the VPO.

It is therefore important to correctly assess one actor's own capabilities and those of others to correlate them with the current situation, forecast the situation, and on the basis of that forecast, make full use of the actor's available potential. Thus, the somewhat inaccurate assessment of the VPO in the Balkans that was made by [North Atlantic Treaty Organization (NATO)] experts on the eve of combat actions in Yugoslavia led to an overestimation of the political and military capabilities of the bloc to resolve the conflict, a downplaying of the role of Russia in the resolution of problems in the Balkans, and an [overall] underestimation of the degree of Russian influence on processes that are taking place in the modern world.

Military-political actions—which could be of a hard military nature or could take the form of peacekeeping activity—are a factor that forms the entire complex of military-political relations (spiritual and material).

What are the primary conditions of the VPO and what are the criteria for its assessment?

For a correct analysis and assessment of the VPO, it is important to establish a clear scale of its possible conditions and criteria, which facilitate a determination. The condition of the VPO can be classified based on concepts such as variability (resiliency)—stable and unstable—or the degree (level) of tension in relations between subjects.

The military-political situation is considered stable (resilient) if the main characteristics of the factors that compose it remain relatively constant. That is, the same subjects (political forces) cooperate (oppose each other); their intentions, objectives, plans, and doctrines do not substantively change; there is not a sharp buildup of military power or a change in the composition of military blocs; in general, the present correlation of forces is preserved; and there are not drastic shifts in the actions of the sides.

The following typical VPO conditions [categories] are based on the degree of tension in relations between various forces:

- **Calm (normal) situation:** built on the legal foundation in line with signed treaties and agreements, trust measures being implemented, cooperation expanding
- **Worsening (tense) situation:** characterized by deterioration of political and then other relations, growth in mistrust, increase in confrontation, reduction of exchanges or negotiations, increase of attacks in the media, increase in military preparations
- **Crisis situation:** characterized by a sharp deterioration of relations as a result of confrontational actions by one of the sides, direct threats of the use of military force (usually accompanied by cessation of talks, the violation of previously signed agreements, and an uptick of "psychological warfare")
- **Military conflict:** relations move outside existing treaties and diplomatic norms; military actions of limited scale occurring
- **War.**

In assessing the VPO, it is important to consider that six phases are observed on the path to military conflict: secret initiation of conflict, increase in tensions, start of the use of force, crisis, military actions (resolution of crisis), and restoration of peace.

In the first phase, which is characterized by the appearance of differences in interests between subjects of the VPO, the situation becomes unstable and military danger increases, although there is not a direct military threat. In the second phase of the conflict, the differences evolve and worsen, turning into contradictions. Those sides with differences turn into adversaries. Confrontation begins and is accompanied by harsh political rhetoric and, at times, by threats and a demonstration of military force. However, the strategic situation can for a

time remain stable. The aforementioned phases [phases 1 and 2] therefore can be characterized as conditions of the VPO, such as potential
military danger.

The third phase coincides with the start of the use of force in a
conflict. Despite the increased chance of a direct military threat, the
strategic situation can still be relatively stable. This period of the development of the VPO can be characterized as a specific military threat
[*napravlennaia voennaia ugroza*].

The fourth phase, which is the most severe, is a crisis condition of
the VPO in which there is a direct military threat. In the majority of
cases, the strategic situation becomes unstable.

The fifth phase of the conflict is tied to its resolution. The crisis,
or high point of tension of the VPO, can be resolved through the
achievement of a compromise or by military force. The VPO in the
conditions of war has the sharp features of confrontation in all directions. Relations are clearly defined: enemy, ally, neutral party.

The sixth phase is the restoration of peace and stability of the
VPO (e.g., withdrawal of troops, transition of states to peacetime
activities).

The conditions listed previously should not necessarily be seen
as mandatory stages of the development of a military conflict. Various
factors have an impact on the military-political process; in particular, the factor of randomness plays a not-insignificant role. Furthermore, the opposing and cooperating sides, as a rule, do not reveal their
cards. Employing various forms and methods of information confrontation, [the sides] disguise true intentions and actual capabilities to ful-
fill them, and they seek to conduct military-political actions using the
factor of surprise.

A sharp transition from externally normal relations toward military conflict has occurred several times over the past decades. This
happened with relations between Iraq and Iran in 1980, with Britain
and Argentina in 1982, and with [the former] Yugoslavia and NATO
countries in 1999. International conflicts in the former Republic of
Yugoslavia and the USSR were characterized by a sharp transition from
peace to military clashes. There is also the opposite case; in 1962, the
USSR and the United States found themselves on the brink of nuclear

war [during the Cuban missile crisis]. Only at the last moment, thanks to the political-diplomatic measures taken by both sides, was a compromise achieved. Displaying the necessary restraint and wisdom, the leadership of the countries met each other halfway and resolved the Cuban missile crisis and normalized relations of the two leading world powers.

The assessment of the VPO is conducted in dialectical unity at the strategic, operational, and tactical levels with participation of the relevant circle of officials (of the state and military). The current and future (forecasted) assessment of the VPO in the most complete sense is a function, first of all, of the senior political and military organs (their leaders), which on the basis of such an assessment make certain important decisions related to state and military structure. Senior commanders (and other commanders, chiefs) and staffs of all levels are involved in the assessment and forecast of the VPO in one way or another. They do this both consistently and in *ad hoc* fashion, the latter based on a command of the senior officer (for example, in the case of a sharp change in the VPO). In all cases, the results of the assessment of the situation that are made by senior political and military organs are used to the maximum extent possible.

Practice has shown that the higher the rank [echelon] of the combat formation and its staff, the more it is necessary to work independently on the VPO assessment to more accurately and sufficiently assess the strategic, operational, and, at times, tactical situation. The results of the analysis and of the VPO assessment in this case are reflected in the introductory parts of the main guidance documents of the senior commander (other commander, chief) and his staff: in directives, orders, memoranda, and assignments.

In characterizing the necessary qualities and the level of training of the officials of the organs of state and military C2 who conduct the analysis and assessment of the VPO, it is necessary to note the following: The assessment of the VPO is tied to analysis of an enormous quantity of material from the most-diverse areas of civil life and spheres of human activity; that is, many different processes, facts, and events. This necessitates a clear organization of the work, the selection of participants from a number of specialists in the fields of military policy, military economics, weapons and equipment, military organization, informatics, psychology, strategy, operational, art, etc. Without such a specialization of experts and the division of their work, it is not possible to capture all of the elements and factors of the situation or to ensure the proper comprehensiveness and reliability of the assessments.

Besides a high level of professional competence of the specialists that are involved in the VPO assessment, there is another important requirement: [The specialists] should understand the style and methods of the work of the director that is overseeing this demanding work. If this quality is not developed among those doing the analytical work in the higher command staffs, then, as experience has shown, a lot of time will be spent in vain. Moreover, those working within the analytical groups of the organs of state and military command and control must develop the ability to be steadfast in their assessments and conclusions of the situation. People that are capable of not only analyzing the situation but of standing behind their work to challenge their director (if needed) are highly valuable in analytical work. [Tsarina] Ekaterina II pointed out that one should only trust those that have the courage to push back against them.

The leader of the organ of state or military C2, whose functions involve analysis of the VPO or the military situation itself, must pay special attention to whether potential subordinates have the most-needed qualities for analytical work, such as the ability to critically assess information coming in, to not give in to suggestion, and to be confident in oneself. Experience working in senior command staffs has shown that it is not easy to find people that fully possess the afore-mentioned qualities. Psychologists claim that only 15–20 percent of specialists are able to critically assess a large volume of information. At the same time, up to 75 percent are susceptible to suggestion and easily become *manipulated subjects*. The presence of such people is simply unacceptable in the organs responsible for assessing the VPO.

Speaking of the necessity of well-organized work of all of those involved in the assessment of the VPO, it is worth noting that in many military C2 organs, even at high levels, there is still not a center that could generalize and analyze all of the incoming information and that could produce a full representation of the VPO. Unfortunately, the collection, analysis, and generalization of situational data is done according to a specific area (e.g., intelligence, political and psychological situation, political-morale condition, combat capability), and the economic situation is not assessed in a practical way. These separate subject areas can only be merged for the senior commander and the chief of staff in the course of conducting a general assessment of [a potential] situation and forecasting its development in the interests of deciding on a course of action for subordinate troops (forces).

Consequently, a military leader must not only have a particular specialization and be competent in his field, but he must also possess a certain breadth of thinking [and] an ability to process and synthesize a large volume of diverse information. For this, it is necessary to have a sufficiently high level of general theoretical training [and] an understanding of global trends and the nature and specifics of the present moment. A leader must have a uniquely deep sense of responsibility for the production of an accurate and up-to-date VPO assessment that has useful conclusions to substantiate decisions, because miscalculations can nullify any effort. That is why a leader is obligated to personally participate in the analytical work of assessing the VPO; it will allow him to not only gain experience and knowledge but also develop intuition that is often most useful in analysis. In working alongside subordinates, a leader who knows how to think deeply and broadly, always, even in "hot" moments of the work, is tactful and restrained, which can unify the efforts of the most diverse group of specialists working on the VPO assessment.

It is also important for a leader to remember that a significant volume of disinformation will be disseminated by the opposing side, which takes into account the leader's personal (e.g., psychological, professional, moral) qualities. It is not a coincidence that there is the practice of compiling psychological portraits. In the U.S. military, for example, such portraits are compiled down to the division/brigade [*soedinenie*] level. These portraits are used in planning and executing precision (targeted) impact on specific leaders of the opposing sides in both peacetime and in wartime.

Finally, in addition to knowledge and the necessary experience, a leader should be proficient in the [VPO] process and carry it out methodically. In the most general sense, there are three basic stages in studying and assessing the VPO.

The preliminary (preparatory) stage is connected to the decision regarding the organizational, methodological, and calculation [*metod-icheskie*] tasks. During this stage, the object of study is determined (e.g., global, regional, local VPO), the objectives and tasks [to be completed] (current or future assessment of the VPO, purpose of the assessment, questions that require special attention), the circle of contributors [who will be involved] and the organization of their work, the [amount of] time [needed] for carrying out all of the tasks, and the format in which the results of the analysis will be presented.

The primary stage involves the analysis, assessment, and generalization of the military-political situation, the forecast of possible changes in the near and long term, and the practical application of the results of the VPO assessment. There are two sub-processes in this stage—the collection and initial processing of the baseline situational data; and the analysis and assessment of the data, the formation of conclusions (generalization), and the forecast for change in the VPO. These processes are interconnected and move along simultaneously to some extent.

The final stage includes the design and presentation of the obtained results to the relevant state and military C2 organs in the form of a military-political overview, memoranda, and, in some cases, recommendations. This work can be finalized through the inclusion of the obtained results in corresponding documents; this inclusion serves as the foundation for making military-political decisions.

The work on the VPO assessment begins with the collection of the necessary baseline data. The primary sources of the baseline data for analysis and assessment of the VPO can be categorized into four groups. The first are the official public documents of state organs, including military and influential civil organizations (e.g., speeches of leaders, announcements, declarations, appeals, manifestos, official notes). Special attention is paid to military doctrines, directives, and orders of the military-political leadership. The second group includes information and communication materials that touch on various spheres of public life, including military issues or problems that are openly published by relevant agencies. The third group consists of mass media reports (e.g., newspapers, journals, radio, television) and [information from] the internet. These sources contain the most up-to-date but also the most contradictory information. Special *information leaks* can be pushed out through the mass media, as [can] propaganda campaigns intended to distract from secret activities and confuse the likely or already declared enemy. Materials collected from mass media, therefore, require a critical eye. The fourth group contains secret materials that are collected by intelligence services and military intelligence.

The initial logical processing of the baseline data involves initially putting them into concise and generally accepted language so that first, the data could be used to compile briefs, and second, that they could be input into a computer. For this, it is necessary to classify and systematize the baseline data. It is important to note that the data and information subject to analysis and assessment not only reflect the VPO beyond the national territory but also concern the situation within the country in the rear of friendly forces. Unfortunately, this part of the VPO assessment often is done superficially and underestimates the possible actions of the enemy in the rear, the appearance of nationalist [or] separatist sentiment, [and so on].

In assessing the VPO, general scientific methods are widely used, such as analysis, synthesis, comparison, generalization, induction, deduction, thought experiments, mathematical methods, [and] factor analysis. Structural models are built both for the military-political situation as a whole as well as for its separate elements.

To identify the best model, research into the [potential] models is done. Subsequently, a final (working) model of the VPO as a whole is created. Using the final VPO model, the trends for change of each element of the VPO and the VPO as a whole are forecasted for the near and long term. Proposals are developed and military-political decisions are made on the basis of the assessment and forecast of the development of the VPO.

The primary objective of the VPO assessment in peacetime is to determine the source and degree of external and internal military dangers. For this, it is necessary to solve a number of analytical tasks related to the identification and assessment of factors that are shaping the VPO at the present time and in the future.

As an example of this, here is a brief analysis (forecast) of the military-political situation in the near term for Russia.

The course of human civilization is on a course of increasing consumption of natural and energy resources. Consequently, at a certain point, there will be a contradiction between the growing demands of the individual, society, and states, and the available reserves of these resources. Moreover, it can be said with confidence that the 21st century will be a century of struggle [among] states for natural resources. Russia, which possesses an enormous amount of reserves of these resources, whether we like it or not, will be pulled into the orbit of global interests of the leading states of the world, who will defend their interests up to and including the use of military force. Thus, if we want to preserve our homeland, without question we must pay serious attention to the issue of ensuring military security of the state and having a military that is capable of repelling any aggression. The war in [the former] Yugoslavia is a grave warning to our state.

It is important to emphasize that the personal traits of the people that drive political processes predetermine the outcome of such processes. Firm political will, a high level of preparation, an equitable temperament, restraint, decisiveness in action, and responsibility in word and deed are all qualities that make the behavior of a political leader predictable and meaningful, which in and of itself facilitates the preservation of stability in the VPO. On the other hand, a low level of professional preparation, a lack of restraint, a proclivity for risk-taking and political bluff, and timidity in making decisions and in actions will quickly have an impact on the condition of military-political relations and make them unpredictable and, as a result, unstable. NATO countries attach great importance to decisiveness and readiness to use all forces and means for the defense of national interests. In the [academic] course on strategy at the U.S. National Defense University, for example, it is said: "If available forces or the determination to use them approaches zero, intimidation [*ustrashenie*] also becomes equal to zero." The presence of such determination is the most important condition for realizing the concept of deterrence [*sderzhivanie*].

Thus the analysis, assessment, and forecast of the military-political situation is a necessary prerequisite for developing and making adequate military-political and purely military (operational-strategic) decisions. Some of the conditions that increase the effectiveness of the assessment and forecast of the VPO are: a sufficiently deep understanding of the nature of military-political relations, the collection of experienced specialists who are experts in a given field, and the precise organization of those experts' work.

The complexity of assessing the VPO requires an objective and critical approach to the obtained results, especially when it comes to the forecast. Forecasts inevitably will be of a probabilistic nature and are presented in the form of model scenarios that reveal possible outcomes of the course of events. All of this emphasizes the need for future development of the methodology for assessing the VPO.

CHAPTER FOUR

On the Quantitative Assessment of the Degree of Military Security

General-Major (ret.) S. R. Tsyrendorzhiev, a senior researcher from the 46th TsNII MOD, presents a methodology for assessing the military security of the state. The approach includes assessing and forecasting tension within the VPO, the degree of military threats, the determination of military power, the potential of general-purpose forces based on combat potential values, and strategic deterrence tools to ensure the military security of Russia.[1]

Decisionmaking on measures for ensuring the military security of the state should be based on the results of an assessment of existing and future military threats and the degree of effectiveness of countering threats through recommended actions. The application of scientifically developed indicators of military security undoubtedly will improve the justification and quality of executing military planning tasks related to force structure and the development of the Armed Forces, other forces [i.e., as of 2016, the National Guard], [executive] organs, and enterprises of the defense-industrial complex, all of which comprise the military organization of the Russian Federation.

The methodological basis for the development of methods for the quantitative assessment of military security is the definition of this concept in the Military Doctrine: "Military security of the Russian Federation (hereafter—military security) is the condition of protection

---

[1]   [Tsyrendorzhiev, 2014.]

of the vital interests of the individual, society, and the state from external and internal military threats resulting from the use of force or the threat of use of force that is characterized by the absence of a military threat or the capability to counter a military threat."[2]

We will consider the details of this definition.

Obviously, a condition of protection of the vital interests of the individual, society, and the state exists when either the state is able to withstand a military threat or in the absence of a military threat.

In accordance with the spirit of the definition of military security, it is logical to think that the formation of such conditions can be achieved in at least three ways:

- the forceful elimination of the enemy himself as a potential source of a military threat or as an actor in an existing dispute, the exacerbation of which has caused a military threat
- convincing the enemy of the futility of employing forceful measures to achieve his military-political objectives because the enemy recognizes the unacceptably high cost of obtaining the desired result—the risk of military and political defeat
- the elimination of the source of threats, which are the result of various types of contradictions in interstate relations.

One does not need evidence to prove the idea that the assurance of military security can be achieved through military (or other forces) and nonmilitary measures, which is especially true in modern conditions.

The concept of *military security* is defined through another concept—military threat. It is clear that the more acute the threat, the larger its scale, and the greater its degree, the lower the level of military security. *Military security*, in essence, is an assessment of the possible influence of a military threat on the territorial integrity and sovereignty of the state and on the ability to realize the vital interests of the state, society, and the individual.

---

[2] Government of the Russian Federation, "Military Doctrine of the Russian Federation," February 5, 2010.

A military threat, as well as a military danger, arises as a result of an increase in tension in the VPO and is an indicator of the interaction of states (coalition of states, or other political actors) in the conduct of their respective military policies.

Analysis of the process of a buildup of tension in the VPO has shown that the essence of this process is found in the substance and scale of military dangers and military threats. In other words, an increase in the tension of the VPO is accompanied by a greater probability of an exacerbation in military-political relations and the potential for a conflict of interests. The situation is characterized by an evolving possibility that opposing sides could resort to the use of force.

The *VPO* can be defined as the result of the interaction of military-political actors conducting military policies in pursuit of national interests.

A natural feature of the VPO is continuous change in the level of tension. An unexpected, abrupt change in the hostility of the situation [*konfliktnost' obstanovki*] occurs only in the speculative phase of assessing the situation, when the military-political leadership of the state is not able to have a clear understanding of the actual condition of affairs or identify trends in the future development of military-political relations with other states, particularly with geopolitical rivals.

To hedge against the influence of such uncertainty, usually some scale is used for assessing typical levels of tension in relations between VPO actors [*sub"ekty VPO*], in accordance with which one can distinguish between several conditions of the military-political situation in peacetime: calm, tense, crisis, conflict. In the case of further escalation of tension in the VPO, a military threat can transition into an armed conflict . . . which, given the increased level of the confrontation, signifies a transition to a wartime military-political situation.

To characterize the VPO, as well as the degree of military danger (or threat), we selected the conflict potential indicator (P_K), which reflects the essence of tension in relations between VPO subjects.

Depending on the degree of generalization in the analysis of the VPO, the conflict potential indicator can vary.

Generalized conflict potential (P_{KO}) is an indicator to measure the degree of VPO tension that depends on the level of military danger and military threat. To characterize the tension in the VPO with the help of such an indicator an ordinal scale is used along with a range of values (PKO) for the proposed VPO conditions. . . .

This linear scale approach for the condition of the military-political situation is wholly appropriate for the execution of practical assessments. It is a variant of similar scales.[3]

The true objectives of military policy of states and other military-political actors are often not known to the international community. Various methods for carrying out military policy can be used to achieve those objectives, not least of which includes methods to confuse the enemy. Analysis of the foreign and domestic policy of a VPO actor

Table 4.1.
Condition of the Military-Political Situation and Assessment Criteria

VPO Condition	Criteria for VPO Assessment
Calm: Peaceful, neighborly, partner, or even friendly relations between sides; absence of military danger or danger is quite low. Military threats are not developing.	$0 \leq P_{KO} \leq 0.5$
Tense: Disputes between sides over some issue(s) arise and intensify; *potential military danger or military threat developing.*	$0 \leq P_{KO} \leq 1$
Crisis: Sharp deterioration of relations. *Actual military danger developing, military threat* arises with possibility for outbreak of military conflict; *possibility of war.*	$1 \leq P_{KO} \leq 2$
Conflict: The use of weapons on a limited scale. *Military danger and military threat present.* There is the direct possibility of outbreak of military conflict; *high probability of war.*	$2 \leq P_{KO} \leq 3$
Military Clash: Primary characteristics of the situation: content, scale, and course of military actions; possibility and condition for ceasing the military conflict or expanding it; factors influencing the course and outcome.	$P_{KO} > 3$

[3]   D. O. Rogozin, ed., *War and Peace in Terms and Definitions*, 2004; V. I. Annenkov, S. N. Baranov et al., *Security of Russia: Geopolitical and Military-Political Aspects*, RUSAVIA, 2006.

can be conducted only on the basis of known information. It is therefore not possible to claim with full certainty that the true military-political objectives of a state will be uncovered as a result of [this kind of] analysis.

Consequently, during the analysis of the substance and character of foreign policy actions taken by this or that actor, one can only speak of the intentions that, to some degree, could be confrontational, conflictual, provocative, opportunistic, as well as neutral, peaceful, or friendly. For the assessment and forecast of the VPO, the primary indicators are therefore taken as the following:

- *generalized conflict potential of intentions (P_{KNO})*: an indicator to measure the degree of tension in the VPO determined by the military policies of military-political actors (measured in the linear scale P_{KO})
- *partial conflict potential of intentions (P_{KNi})*: an indicator to measure the degree of tension in relations of VPO actors in i spheres of military policy (measured in the linear scale P_{KO})
- *level of conflict potential in the j-th element of the VPO (P_{KNij})*: an indicator that characterizes the degree of conflict potential of j events or actions by the actor (coalition) in the *i-th* sphere (measured in the linear scale P_{KO}).

The value of level of hostility of the *j-th* element of the VPO should be assessed in the course of analysis of the primary parameters and indicators characterizing the situation within the confines of the conflict situation under consideration. The given parameters should be organized in groups that correlate to the primary areas of activity of states. . . .

Each of the parameters of the VPO, respectively, are characterized by a system of indicators. They can accept concrete values. For example, with regard to the military sphere the policies of a state interacting with the Russian Federation, five parameters of VPO tension are considered. One of them, such as the activity of countries in the realm of information confrontation [*informatsionnoe protivoborstvo*], is characterized by two indicators: the level of organizational-technical support of the information confrontation and the condition of the information confrontation.

The indicators of tension, based on analysis of actions of subjects of international law, can have a limited set of values. . . . It is believed that the given values of tension in the VPO represent a whole group of possible options of actions by a considered actor. The principles of the aforementioned approach for the analysis of tension in the VPO were developed by officers in the Main Operations Directorate of the General Staff of the Armed Forces of the Russian Federation: Captain 1st Rank A. V. Dikii and Colonel K. O. Peschanenko, and certified [*aprobirovany*] in the course of operational training events.

The chosen indicators (P_{KNO}) describe the level of hostility of intentions of the military-political leadership of a VPO actor. But intentions can be deliberately provocative [*provokatsionnye*] or opportunistic. Do these intentions represent an actual threat? What is the scale of this threat? The answer to these questions can be obtained through an assessment of the military power [*voennaia moshch'*] of the source of the military threat. It is generally accepted that military-economic potential and military-economic power, which themselves are based on the economic potential and economic power of a country, make up the material base that ensures military security.

However, in the assessment of military challenges and threats to military security, one should consider indicators such as *military-economic power*—the real capability of an economy to satisfy the demands of the military organization of the state, the strategic deterrence forces and the general-purpose forces, and *military power*—the aggregate of all the material and spiritual forces constantly activated in peacetime and wartime, and the capability of the state to mobilize all these forces for the conduct of war (or to repel aggression). The generalized framework for the formation of military power is shown. . . .

Clearly, a VPO actor that possesses military power superior to that of Russia is potentially a source of a military threat. The realization of this threat depends on many factors: the political will of the leadership of the actor (state), the degree of popularity of the leadership's policy among society, and several others. Nevertheless, the cor-

Figure 4.1
Structure for the Analysis of the Military-Political Situation

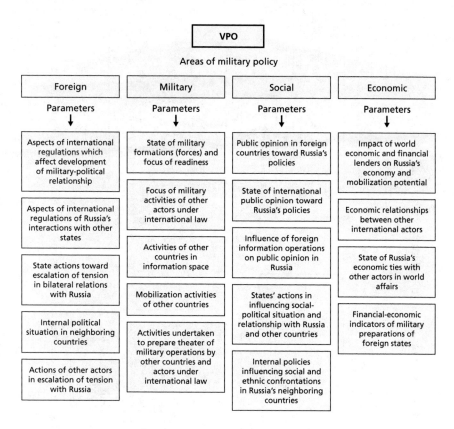

relation of military power of actors can serve as an indicator of the capability of a VPO actor to realize political intentions vis-à-vis Russia.

In the case of a military power correlation in favor of a potential enemy and an enemy's hostile intentions, a military threat [could become] quite serious. Conversely, given a military power correlation in favor of Russia, the hostile intentions of an enemy [could] turn out to lack substance, [could be] opportunistic, or [could be] tied to the military might of allies, which would force [Russia] to consider the broader makeup of the opposing coalition.

Figure 4.2
The Relationship of Parameters and Indicators of Tension in the Military-Political Situation

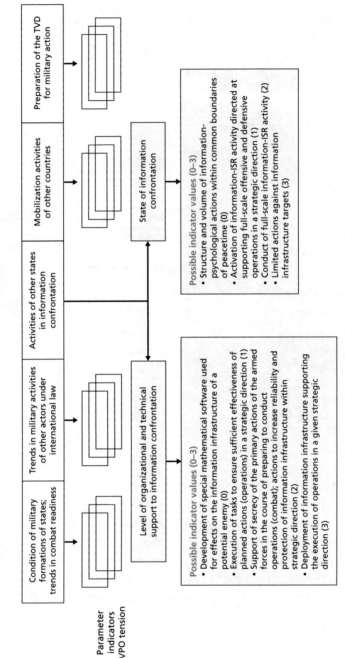

[NOTE: TVD = theater of military operations; ISR = intelligence, surveillance, and reconnaissance. The figure has been slightly altered for clarity with no change to content.]

Figure 4.3
Generalized Framework of the Formation of the Military Power of the State

Military power: The aggregate of all material and spiritual forces that are constantly activated in peacetime and wartime; the capability of the state to mobilize all forces for the conduct of war (to repel aggression).

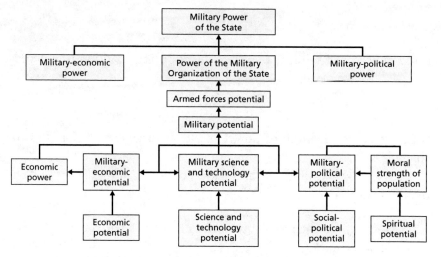

[NOTE: Figure slightly altered for clarity with no change to content.]

Therefore, it is proposed that the correlation of military power be added to the list of primary factors that lead to a military threat, along with such factors as military-political intentions and the degree of aggressiveness. [It is also] proposed to introduce a corresponding indicator—the conflict potential of the correlation of military power (P_S). The conflict potential of intentions and the conflict potential of the correlation of military power are the potentials that influence actual military-political tension, which is measured with the indicator for generalized conflict potential (P_{KO}).

We consider an example of the analytical dependencies for the calculation of selected indicators.

The degree of superiority of one actor over others in aggregate power S is calculated with the formula:

$$S = \frac{MP_G^{Coal}}{MP_G^{RF}}$$

where

$$MP_G^{Coal}$$

is the indicator of military power of the opposing coalition (state) and

$$MP_G^{RF}$$

is the indicator of military power of the Russian Federation and its allies.

Generally speaking, the correlation of power of the sides can have the following values:

- $S \leq 0.3$ (overwhelming superiority of the Russian Federation over the other side)
- $0.3 < S \leq 0.5$ (superiority of the Russian Federation over the other side)
- $0.5 < S \leq 0.9$ (some superiority of the Russian Federation over the other side)
- $0.9 < S \leq 1.1$ (approximate parity of aggregate power of the sides)
- $1.1 < S \leq 2$ (some superiority of the other side over the Russian Federation)
- $2 < S \leq 3$ (superiority of the other side over the Russian Federation and its allies)
- $S > 3$ (overwhelming superiority of the other side over the Russian Federation).

The indicator S is transformed into the indicator "conflict potential of the correlation of military power," and the values of S are recalculated into the aforementioned scale of conflict potential . . . taking into account the fact that the superiority of VPO subjects over others in aggregate power is, for some, a factor of deterrence against the out-

Table 4.2
Assessment of the Conflict Potential of the Correlation of Aggregate Power of VPO Actors

Indicator	Normative Value	Assessment of the Conflict Potential of the Correlation of Military Power of VPO Actors
Overwhelming superiority of the Russian Federation over the other side	$S \leq 0.3$	$P_s = -3$
Superiority of the Russian Federation over the other side	$0.3 < S \leq 0.5$	$P_s = -2$
Some superiority of the Russian Federation over the other side	$0.5 < S \leq 0.9$	$P_s = -1$
Approximate parity of aggregate power of the sides	$0.9 < S \leq 1.1$	$P_s = 0$
Some superiority of the other side over the Russian Federation	$1.1 < S \leq 2$	$P_s = 1$
Superiority of the other side over the Russian Federation	$2 < S \leq 3$	$P_s = 2$
Overwhelming superiority of the other side over the Russian Federation	$S > 3$	$P_s = 3$

break of war, while for others it is a factor that increases the probability of using military force in pursuit of national interests.

The values of generalized conflict potential (*PKO*) can be defined as a function of two primary variables:

$$P_{KO} = \left(P_{KNO}; P_S \right)$$

The generalized indicator PKO can be calculated with the following dependency:

0, if $P_{KNO} + P_S \leq 0$,

$$P_{KO} = \left\{ \frac{P_{KNO} + P_s}{2} \right\},$$

if $P_{KNO} + PS > 0$.

In the assessment of the VPO, it is appropriate to initially include within military power (MP_G) only the indicators of combat capabilities of the armed forces: the combat potentials of force groupings deployed in a given region, beginning with permanently ready units. If it is not possible to neutralize the military threat with these forces, it is necessary to consider the combat potentials of force groupings of the armed forces during partial and full mobilization, and, finally, the total military power of the state. That is, in the assessment of the generalized conflict potential indicator at the local level (S):

$$S = \frac{\Sigma_{i=1}^{I} CP_{AFj}}{\Sigma_{j=1}^{J} CP_{AFPRUi}}$$

where CP_{AFj} is the combat potential of the j force grouping deployed in the considered direction, CP_{AFPRUi} is the combat potential of the force grouping consisting of [Russian] permanently ready units deployed in the considered direction; in the assessment of the generalized conflict potential at the regional level (a single strategic [operational]) direction:

$$S = \frac{\Sigma_{i=1}^{I} CP_{AFj}}{\Sigma_{j=1}^{J} CP_{MAFRFi}}$$

where CP_{MAFRFi} is the combat potential of the [Russian] force grouping deployed in the considered direction after partial or full mobilization; in the assessment of the generalized conflict potential at the global level and a separate large region:

$$S = \frac{\Sigma_{i=1}^{I} MP_{Gi}}{\Sigma_{j=1}^{J} MP_{Gj}}$$

where MP_{Gi} is the military power of i state, and MP_{Gj} is the military power of j state.

The calculation of the generalized conflict potential, taking into account the conflict potential of intentions and the potential of the correlation of military power, provides a more objective assessment of the degree of tension in the VPO, [as well as] the degree and scale of the military threat, which we suggest to measure using an indicator such as the *potential of military threat* (P_{MT}). The composition of the dependence of the potential of military threat on the sizes of the military power of the state allows for the determination of the degree of influence of the values of the combat potential of this state on the military threat. Assessments of the possibility of force to parry the military threat can thus be performed, as well as assessments ([using] a range of values) of the contribution of nonmilitary measures—e.g., economic, political-diplomatic—to the execution of this task [of mitigating military threats].

To obtain more-complete and accurate results in the assessment of military (force) measures to mitigate the military threat, [one must] consider factors of military strategic deterrence, the primary contribution to which are actions of nuclear and nonnuclear deterrence.

The factor of nonnuclear deterrence in modern conditions, like the factor of nuclear deterrence, can produce desired effects only under the condition of the guaranteed capability of the armed forces of the Russian Federation to parry the threat of disarming strikes by enemy forces primarily through the [Russian] capability to disrupt (repel) the air (aerospace, air-sea) attack of the enemy. [This capability] can be considered a factor of strategic deterrence against the outbreak (or escalation) of aggression against the Russian Federation.

Using such a conception of strategic deterrence, one can presume that the danger of the outbreak of large-scale war or the escalation of a limited regional (local) war into a large-scale war is significantly neutralized through strategic deterrence. Nevertheless, one should objectively assess the real impact and conditions for achieving both nuclear [and] nonnuclear deterrence.

We consider the quantitative expression of the influence of strategic deterrence and the conditions for achieving it in an example of the calculation of the conflict potential of the correlation of military power.

The potential of strategic deterrence (P_{SD}) must be such that it would be possible to neutralize the maximum values of the value indicator of tension in the military-political situation (P_{KO})—the condition of a military threat (P_{MT}) corresponding to the absence of a military danger in the VPO. The minimal values of this indicator show the impossibility of inflicting damage to the critically important objects of the enemy that disrupts [the enemy's] existential activity and the primary functions of the state and society. The normative values of P_{SD} are presented . . . .

As noted previously, the capability of the armed forces of the Russian Federation to mitigate threats of strikes (P_{MT}) of strategic non-nuclear weapons of the enemy is a key condition in achieving strategic deterrence. Obviously, the values of this indicator (P_{MT}), which characterizes the influence of such a condition on strategic nuclear deterrence, must be found within the boundaries of the interval 0–1 (the normative values of P_{MT} are shown . . .).

In this case, the resultant values of the potential of strategic deterrence (P_{SDR}) can be assessed with the following dependency:

$$P_{SDR} = P_{SD} * P_{MT}$$

Table 4.3
Normative Values of Strategic Deterrence Potential

Indicator	Assessment of Strategic Deterrence Potential
Russia is capable of inflicting guaranteed unacceptable damage against the enemy	$P_{SD} = 3$
Russia is capable of guaranteed destruction of the primary critically important military targets	$P_{SD} = 2$
Russia is capable of guaranteed destruction of individual critically important military targets	$P_{SD} = 1$
Russia is not capable of guaranteed destruction of critically important military targets	$P_{SD} = 0$

Military conflicts of a lesser intensity and smaller scale must be localized and extinguished with general-purpose force groupings of the Russian armed forces in any strategic direction. In this regard, the means and methods of strategic nonnuclear deterrence can be employed to inflict (or threaten to inflict) unacceptable damage to critically important targets on the territory of the aggressor. However, in this case, the considerable nonmilitary losses that will accompany strikes by the nonnuclear means of strategic deterrence require a thorough understanding of the necessity and timing of the employment of such assets.

Relatedly, in wartime, one of the most important tasks of the force groupings of the armed forces of the Russian Federation along strategic axes is, by taking decisive actions, to not allow a situation to get to a point that requires taking radical strategic deterrence measures[;] in peacetime, one of the tasks is to remove any doubt from potential enemies regarding [Russia's] sufficient capabilities to successfully repel an armed attack. In any case, the enemy, in determining the correlation between the desired and possible outcome of a war of choice, must

Table 4.4
The Normative Values of the Indicator of Threat Mitigation of Strikes of Strategic Nonnuclear Forces of the Enemy

Indicator	Assessment of P_{MT}
Mitigation of threats of strikes of strategic nonnuclear forces of the enemy with high level of certainty	$0.8 < P_{MT} \leq 1$
Mitigation of threats of strikes of strategic nonnuclear forces of the enemy in general is ensured	$0.6 < P_{MT} \leq 0.8$
Strikes of strategic nonnuclear forces of the enemy can be weakened	$0.4 < P_{MT} \leq 0.6$
Mitigation of threats of strikes of strategic nonnuclear forces of the enemy is not ensured	$0.2 < P_{MT} \leq 0.4$
The capability to mitigate threats of strikes of strategic nonnuclear forces of the enemy does not exist	$P_{MT} < 0.2$

always come to the conclusion that the price is unacceptably high and that there is a risk of military and political defeat.

The analytical dependency for the calculation of a potential military threat (P_{MT}) at the global level, [the level of] large-scale war, and [the level of] local war is the following:

$$P_{MT} = \begin{cases} P_{KO} + P_{SDR}, & if \to P_{KO} \geq P_{SDR}; \\ 0, & if \to P_{KO} < P_{SDR} \end{cases}$$

From the aforementioned dependency, it is clear that cases are considered in which the strategic deterrence potential in the aforementioned scale can exceed the values of conflict potential. This situation conditionally means that the potential of a military threat is reduced to zero.

Based on analysis, military security directly depends on the presence and value of the potential of a military threat. It should be kept in mind that the indicators presented in this article cannot play the roles of precise analytical tools for each of the discussed factors. [The indicators] characterize their most common features in terms of assessing military security. The task of assessing the military-political situation cannot be done precisely because of the significant degree of uncertainty in the assessment. Accordingly, the assessment of many of the baseline characteristics of the parameters of the areas of the VPO is done through expert elicitation, albeit in a unified scale.

One can assert that military security as a condition of protection is a psychological assessment of the value of the potential of a military threat. Experimental design theory methods have been some of the most successful in connecting numerical values of the parameters of the properties of an object and the quality of an object together. It is therefore suggested to apply a Harrington's desirability function.[4] As it relates to our task, the function of dependency of military security on the potential of a military threat $b_{ko} = f(P_{MT})$ will be the following:

---

[4] Iu. P. Adler, E. V. Markova, and Iu. V. Granovskii, *Experiment Planning in the Search for Optimal Conditions*, Moscow: Nauka, 1976.

$$b_{ko} = 1 - \exp\left(-\exp\left(-\left(Y_{min} + \frac{\left(P_{MT} - P_{MTmin}\right) * \left(Y_{max} - Y_{min}\right)}{P_{MTmax} - P_{MTmin}}\right)\right)\right)$$

where:

Y_{max} is the maximum value of the conditional scale of the desirability function, equal to "6";

Y_{min} is the minimum value of the conditional scale of the desirability function, equal to "-3";

P_{MTmax} is the maximum value of the scale of the values of the potential of a military threat, equal to "3";

P_{MTmin} is the minimum value of the scale of the values of the potential of a military threat, equal to "0".

Based on the calculations, we obtain values of the psychological assessment of the degree of military danger, which we propose to spread out along a broad, spatial five-level scale.

Based on the analysis of the calculations of the influence of the correlation of military power of the Russian Federation and a confrontational VPO actor on the military security of Russia, given various values of strategic deterrence potential (*PSDR*) and the values of the conflict potential of intentions, one can see that the greater the tension in relations between Russia and a selected VPO actor, the higher the potential of military threat and the lower the achieved level of military security in a given correlation of military power of the sides.

The capabilities of strategic deterrence forces have a consequential influence on military security. [Figure] presents the results of the assessment of military security given a maximum potential of military threat (P_{MT} = 3) and a superiority in military power (taking into account only general-purpose forces) of the opposing side of 5–6 times (b_{ko3}), 2–3 times (b_{ko2}), and practically even capabilities of the general-purpose forces (b_{ko1}). Thus, given the capability to inflict unacceptable damage and to destroy the most important military targets of the probable enemy or source of military threat, the military security of Russia is ensured even against an opponent with overwhelming superiority in military power.

Figure 4.4
Assessment of the Dependence of Military Security on the Potential of a Military Threat

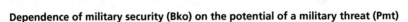

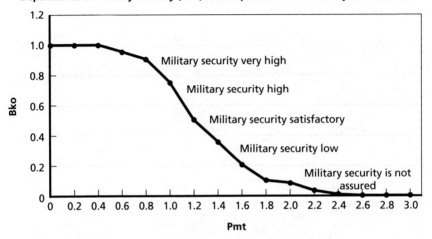

Dependence of military security (Bko) on the potential of a military threat (Pmt)

[NOTE: Figure slightly altered for clarity with no change to content.]

In addition, the proposed methodological approach sets out a range of influence of nonmilitary measures. As calculations have shown, to ensure military security at a level of at least 0.8 ("very high") in the absence of strategic deterrence, the allowable ratio of military power in favor of the enemy, depending on the size of the conflict potential of the intentions of the enemy, can vary from 1.1 to 2.2 in favor of the enemy. With a value of strategic deterrence potential $P_{SDR} = 1$, this range expands to 1.1 to 4.2; at $P_{SDR} = 2$, 3 to 6.2.

Therefore, with the baseline data, such as the results of the assessment of the condition of the military-political situation, as well as the capabilities of [Russia's] strategic deterrence forces, it is possible to calculate the required correlation of military power of the sides depending on the success of nonmilitary measures in reducing the aggressive intentions of the enemy. [It is also possible, with these data] to find the requirements for reducing the conflict potential of the enemy's intentions in those areas of military-political relations where tension is increased.

Figure 4.5
Assessment of the Dependence of Military Security on Strategic Deterrence Potential

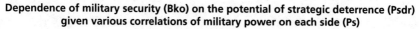

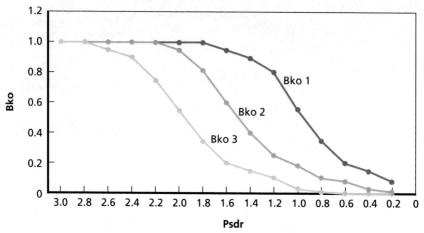

Dependence of military security (Bko) on the potential of strategic deterrence (Psdr) given various correlations of military power on each side (Ps)

[NOTE: Figure slightly altered for clarity with no change to content.]

The proposed approach facilitates the analysis of trends in the domestic and foreign policy of VPO actors and helps to identify contradictions in their relations and to determine the sources of military threats. This, in turn, can produce recommendations directed at the reduction of tension in the military-political situation and strengthening of cooperation between states.

The important functions that can be accomplished with the proposed methodological approach are the assessment of the degree of correspondence of the combat composition of force groupings of the armed forces of the Russian Federation that are deployed in strategic directions and of strategic deterrence forces in assuring military security. This method also allows for the determination of the contribution of the force component of strategic deterrence to national security.

CHAPTER FIVE

Forecast of the Military Dangers and Threats to Russia

The article presents the results of a collaborative study involving the 46th TsNII MOD and a number of Russian academic institutions that conduct research on national security and defense issues. The purpose of the study, apparently conducted in 2014, was to forecast not only military threats to Russia but their nature and probability in 2030 and 2045. Researchers applied parts of the methodology described in the preceding article, such as various VPO scenario forecasts, to offer different potential geopolitical conditions through which to forecast possible military threats.[1]

The starting point in the organization of activity of the state in assuring military security is the assessment and forecast of the external and internal political situation[s], [their] military-political aspects, and the possible military dangers and threats that could occur as a result.

This article is devoted to the presentation of the results related to the resolution of the above task [assessment and forecast of dangers and threats] that were obtained through the work of a scientific collective from MGTU, the Moscow State Institute of International Relations, Moscow State University, [and] the Institute of the United States and Canada, with the 46th TsNII MOD playing a coordinating role.[2]

---

[1] [Tsyrendorzhiev, 2015.]

[2] This article is an abridged version. For the full text, see Russian Academy of Missile and Artillery Sciences, *Works of the All-Russia Scientific-Practical Conference on "Current Problems in Defense and Security,"* Vol. 3: *Arms and Military Equipment*, St. Petersburg, 2015.

The research considered forecasted indicator values for the development of countries around the world in socio-economic, demographic, and scientific-technical contexts[.] The forecasted indicator values were derived by specialists from the research organizations of the Ministry of Economic Development and the Russian Academy of Sciences.

The dominant trend in global development is the attempt by several countries to actively lay claim to their interests in the international arena, [and] to increase their roles in the international division of labor, in the consumption of resources, in the formation of global policy, and in the monitoring and control of the rules of global development. A first-order issue is the struggle of new leaders for the preservation of national traditions and values as an alternative to the "liberal" values of the Anglo-Saxon civilization. A methodologically important trend is the definitive influence of the factors of global political development on the process of socioeconomic development of countries in the forecasted period.

Starting from a large number of possible variants for the interaction of global and regional leaders, it seems wholly justified to select the most-probable scenarios for the development of the international situation, the name and description of which are presented . . . .

The situation we observe at the present time [2015] most closely resembles the scenario "harsh globalization," which supposes the unquestioned dominance of the United States, although the transformation of the modern world order into a less America-centric one is quite possible in the near future. The point of bifurcation, the emergence of which was caused by the crises in Ukraine, the Middle East, and North Africa, with uncontrolled migration of masses of people into Europe, will be overcome. As a result of the joint efforts of the international community, this transition can lead to new, more favorable conditions for the development of new actors in global politics.

Assessment of the Probability of the Scenarios of the Development of the International Situation

The assessment of the probability of the scenarios of the development of the international situation was conducted through an expert-analytical method. Experts assessed the preferability of this or that scenario on the basis of which probability assessments were obtained for the development of the international situation. To justify the assessments, a logical schema was used. . . . The assessment probability results are shown . . . which were obtained through a constructed graph.

In sum, the most probable scenarios are the following:

- to 2030: "Moderate globalization—Prolonged America-centrism" and, somewhat less probable, "Bipolarity 2.0." Another possibility is instead of the scenario "Bipolarity 2.0," the scenario "Moderate globalization—Hierarchical polycentrism."
- To 2045: "Moderate globalization—Hierarchical polycentrism" and, becoming less probable, "Bipolarity 2.0." Another possibility, as a result of a financial, economic, or political crisis, is the "Regionalization—Deglobalization" scenario in place of "Bipolarity 2.0."

The distribution of assessments of "favorability" for the Russian Federation in international situation scenarios is shown . . . .

Conclusions from the Assessment of the International Situation Development Forecast

The conditions for the development of Russia up to 2030 within the bounds of the most probable international situation scenarios in general can be characterized as "average" in terms of degree of favorability for Russia. By the end of the next forecast period, conditions for Russian development, regardless of the realization of one of the probable scenarios, could be characterized from "above average" to "high" in terms of favorability to Russia.

Figure 5.1
Primary Scenarios for the Development of the International Situation

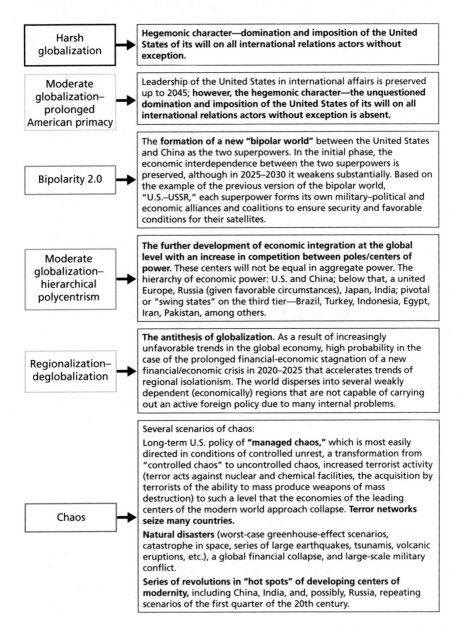

Assurance of the realization of such a combination of scenarios is possible under a number of conditions, the most important of which are: the resolution of tasks for new industrialization, to strengthen and develop the socio-political potential of the state through effective socially oriented domestic policy, and the preservation and development of fundamental moral values of the nation. This will ensure the important and growing role of Russia in the formation and strengthening of trade, economic, and military coalitions and alliances with the leading states of the world that conduct independent policies and pursue their national interests within the bounds of international law.

If Russia does not manage to create the aforementioned conditions, it will not have a substantive role in the formation of new power centers, nor will it be able to influence the international situation. The

Figure 5.2
Logical Schema (Graph) for Assessing the Possibility of International Situation Scenario Development to 2030 and 2045

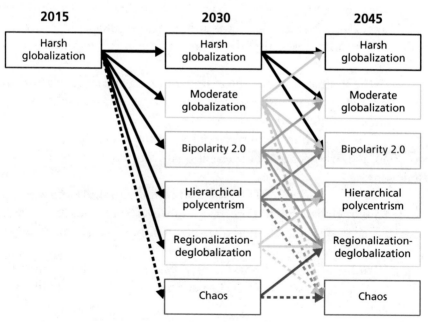

[NOTE: Content slightly condensed for clarity; for full scenario names see Figure 5.1.]

role of Russia in the modern world order is so high that its exit from the stage of the leading actors could sharply change global development trends, and Russia's fate would be unenviable. Economic stagnation [in Russia] will lead to economic crisis, the inevitable rise of internal political instability, the disintegration of Russia, [and] military actions taken against Russia with the aim of seizing parts of its territory that are rich in various natural resources. Conditions for the creation of Eurasian coalitions would also be hindered, BRICS [Brazil, Russia, India, China, South Africa] would disband, [and] allies within the Collective Security Treaty Organization (CSTO) and the Shanghai Cooperation Organization (SCO) would end up under U.S. and NATO influence in some form. China would be relegated to the role of regional power with decreased influence in [both] the Asia-Pacific region and other regions of the world. It is highly possible that, using disputes between India and China, an American administration would manage to attract India into its sphere of influence, which for a long period (most of the 21st century) would shape the global order.

The forecast scenarios of the VPO at the global level, in general, align with the most probable scenarios of geopolitical development to 2030 and 2045. Nevertheless, it is appropriate to independently consider the military-political and military-strategic aspects of the given scenarios.

The key subjects of the forecasted VPO are the leading actors in international relations—the so-called power centers—which are also the sources of military dangers and threats.

In the most likely international situation scenarios [projected] to 2030, the arrangement of international relations actors will be the following.

U.S.-led coalition (NATO, European Union, Japan, Australia): U.S. leadership in global affairs is preserved; however, the United States will not be the hegemon and will not be able to impose its will on all other actors without exception.

Coalition of other actors in international affairs: BRICS countries, the SCO, and Russia and CSTO-participating countries [will be a coalition].

Non-global structure "Hierarchical polycentrism": This structure, despite its obvious stability, will nevertheless attempt to move from hierarchy to polarization through the joining of states in the second and third tier around the poles of power—the United States and China. The bipolar system of the world order could form in such a way.

In each of the proposed scenarios for the global development of the VPO, there are certain idiosyncrasies. However, as a result of the geopolitical position of Russia, the primary military dangers and threats—both at the present time and in the future—will mostly remain unchanged and will be characterized most of all by their level and scale.

Primary Military Dangers and Threats to the Russian Federation to 2030 and 2045

Global military dangers and threats to Russia in the considered forecast period will be tied to the United States and their allies both in the west and in the east. The nature of these threats lies in the possibility of the outbreak of a large-scale war against Russia with the use of nuclear weapons.

Table 5.1
Assessment of the Probability of International Situation Scenarios

Scenario	2030	2045
Harsh globalization	.15	.09
Moderate globalization—prolonged American primacy	.24	.16
Rise of China—Bipolarity 2.0	.19	.24
Moderate globalization—hierarchical polycentrism	.18	.26
Regionalization—deglobalization	.12	.13
Chaos	.12	.12

[NOTE: Harrington scale from 0 to 1; experts must rank probabilities of considered scenarios.]

Table 5.2
Favorability of International Situation Scenarios for Russian Federation

Scenario	Assessment
Harsh globalization	low
Moderate globalization— prolonged American primacy	medium, low-medium
Rise of China—Bipolarity 2.0	high-medium
Moderate globalization— hierarchical polycentrism	high
Regionalization—deglobalization	high
Chaos	low

The source of global military dangers and threats both at the present time and in the future will be the ambitions of Russia's geopolitical rivals:

- to achieve unquestioned domination and to preclude Russia from being a center of power that possesses nuclear weapons
- to turn Russia into a country that is unable to influence the development of international relations in the world and regionally.

The source of global military dangers and threats in the considered forecast period are, without question, the United States and its NATO allies.

With respect to the realization of an international situation scenario in which China becomes the leader of the globalization project [; this] could present a global military threat if Russia is not able to play the role of equal ally, which could happen in the case of an unsuccessful attempt to modernize the Russian national economy.

Military threats and dangers at the regional and local levels will form along the perimeter of the borders of Russia in connection with residual or new disputes with neighbors or other states in regions where Russia has national interests. The exacerbation of these disputes could lead to the outbreak of various military conflicts. The primary danger

Table 5.3
Sources of Military Dangers and Threats at the Regional and Local Levels

Region	Source of Military Danger (Threat)	Source-Actor of Military Danger (Threat)
Arctic	Grievances of other countries against the redistribution of control over hydrocarbon reserves along the Arctic shelf that are harmful to Russian national interests.	United States, NATO countries
West	Territorial grievances of the Baltic states, Poland, and Germany against Russia and Belarus. The ambition of the United States and Western countries to remove a potential geopolitical opponent and create an uninterrupted zone of vassal states in Eastern Europe.	United States, Baltic states, Poland, and Germany
Southwest	The territorial grievances of Ukraine (with the support of the United States and NATO) against Russia; of Azerbaijan (with support of Turkey) against Armenia on the disputed territory of Nagorno-Karabakh; the revanchist intentions of Georgia (with the support of the United States and NATO) to return Abkhazia and South Ossetia to Georgia.	Ukraine, Azerbaijan, and Georgia, all supported by NATO countries
Central Asia	Grievances of Islamic extremist organizations in Central Asia and the Xinjiang Uyghur Autonomous Region of China; the ambition in the North Caucasus and Volga region of Russia to create one or several Islamic states (caliphate), to seize parts of Russian, Chinese and Kazakh territory, and to take power in Tajikistan, Kyrgyzstan, and Uzbekistan.	Islamist extremist organizations; illegal armed groups outside territory of Russia, Kazakhstan, and other countries as well as within them
East	Territorial grievances of Japan on account of the ownership of the Kuril Islands, Sakhalin Island, the Kamchatka Peninsula, and parts of Primorskii Krai.	Japan, United States, South Korea

is in the possibility of escalation of these conflicts into something larger in scale, which is fraught with the possible transition of the opposing sides to the employment of weapons of mass destruction. . . . The significant superiority of China over Russia in the combat potential of force groupings in the Siberian and Far Eastern strategic directions in combination with the second-largest economic potential in the world in and of itself is a military danger for Russia. However, the absence of aggressive intentions among the Chinese military-political leadership, their clear understanding of historical perspectives of full cooperation with Russia, and the sober assessment of Russia's military-strategic capabilities allow for the conclusion of the absence of a military threat that some specialists traditionally have harbored.

A key feature of all types of military threats, to one degree or another, will be their transborder character. Specifically, this involves the broad use of the capabilities of the destructive opposition within Russia, which organizes disruptive behavior among the population through the use of mass media, including the internet, as well as the foreign training and insertion into Russia of pseudo-religious extremist terrorist organizations and quasilegal or illegal armed groups.

Internal Military Dangers and Threats

Internal military dangers and threats are tied to attempts to violently overthrow legally elected authorities and to change the constitutional structure of Russia through preparations and execution of "Bolotnaia-2," or the "Ukraine" scenario, as well as through the desire to separate parts of Russian territory to form an Islamic caliphate.

The sources of internal military dangers and threats are the following:

1. The ambition of the liberal opposition [in Russia] to integrate Russia into the socio-political structures of the West and reconstruct the country under the leading Western socio-cultural values with the support of the United States and NATO countries, who are trying to remove their geopolitical opponent from its leading role in global politics and to create favorable conditions for the exploitation of Russian natural resources.

Figure 5.3
Probability Assessment of the Realization of External Military Threats to Russian Security

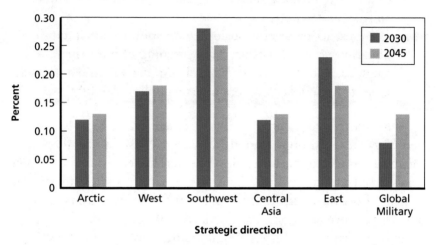

[NOTE: Harrington scale from 0 to 1; experts must rank probabilities of considered events.]

Figure 5.4
Probability Assessment of the Realization of Internal Military Threats to Russian Security

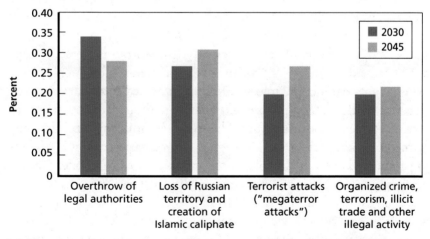

[NOTE: Harrington scale from 0 to 1; experts must rank probabilities of considered events.]

2. The expansion in scale of international terrorism and organized crime, ethnic and religious extremism, the growth of nationalist and separatist movements, [and] the ambition of Islamic organizations to create a Sharia [law] state, the "Islamic Caliphate," on Russian territory.

3. The presence of negative socio-demographic trends and the continuation of social tension, the worsening of interethnic, interreligious, and political-ideological disputes in various Russian subjects [e.g., oblasts, autonomous republics and districts].

The sources of internal military dangers and threats include opposition extremist organizations with a pro-Western liberal orientation and Islamic extremist organizations that use existing or reformed illegal armed groups for their own purposes; terrorist organizations; a system of organizations that transport and sell drugs from the near abroad and beyond; [and] large-scale illegal migration (first of all within large cities), that brings with it the threat of Islamic extremism. . . . [Figures] show the results of probability assessments of the realization of external and internal military dangers and threats to the Russian Federation to 2030 and 2045.

The Nature of Military Threats and Preparation of their Realization

At the present time, there are clear signs that Russia's geopolitical rivals are preparing for the realization of existing and future military threats [to Russia]. The signs include the reform and qualitative rearmament of states [and] the desire of certain developing countries to possess weapons of mass destruction as a means of guaranteeing protection against external aggression. The reform of the U.S. armed forces deserves the closest attention among those activities regarding the preparation of foreign countries to future wars. The American military is being transformed into a unified armed force of the information age; it is becoming more flexible and mobile; more capable of using modern information systems, improved means of intelligence and surveillance, and precision-guided munitions; and in shortened time periods with minimal losses can achieve victory over any opponent. Some of the most important aspects of modern and future military dangers and threats

Table 5.4
The Nature of Military Threats to Russia and the Features of Their Strategic Character

Threat Type	Strategic Direction	Source of Military Threat	Type of Potential Conflict	Primary Characteristics of Military Actions Depending on Range of Forecast Period			
				Up to 5 Years	5–15 Years	15–30 Years	30–50 Years
External military threats	West	Territorial disputes in Baltic region	Armed conflict, local war, regional war, large-scale war	Military actions against high-tech enemy		The role of nuclear weapons as a factor of deterrence is neutralized; military actions against high-tech enemy using breakthrough technologies	
	Southwest	Territorial grievance of Ukraine (over Crimea, Sevastopol)	Armed conflict, local war	Traditional military actions		Military actions against high-tech enemy	
	Central Asia	Unresolved Afghanistan problems, United States attempts to weaken Russia in the region	Armed conflict	Traditional military actions		Military actions against high-tech enemy	
	East	Territorial grievances of Japan	Armed conflict, local war, regional war	Military actions against high-tech enemy		The role of nuclear weapons as a factor of deterrence is neutralized; military actions against high-tech enemy using breakthrough technologies	
	Arctic	Grievances of states regarding natural resources	Armed conflict	Military actions against high-tech enemy			
Internal military threats	Russian territory	Terrorism	Terrorist acts	Special actions within counterterror operations			
	Volga/North Caucasus	Separatism, terrorism	Internal armed conflict	Traditional military actions	Military actions against high-tech enemy		

include the challenge of cyberspace (preparation and conduct of cyber-attacks and cyber operations), the militarization of space, problems in food security, and trends toward the loss of national and civilizational foundations.

An unfavorable outcome that is becoming more probable is the outbreak of one or two internal armed conflicts on Russian territory. These conflicts could be instigated from outside the country. In such a war, the combat actions of the Russian Armed Forces, other forces, and combat formations take on the characteristics of a special operation and would be similar to that of an anti-partisan war with the indirect participation of NATO states and third countries with the local employment of precision-guided munitions. Regardless of the circumstances, the "correct justification" for the objectives and causes of the war will immediately be presented to the international community.

Russia and its allies could be dragged into military conflicts of varying scale, each of which have a number of substantive features that, taken together, form three types of conflicts. These are traditional military actions during the course of which the opposing side is capable of employing weapons and military technologies that were characteristic of the 20th century, high-tech military actions, and military actions against a high-tech enemy using breakthrough technologies in the context of nuclear weapons as a factor of deterrence being neutralized [*nivelirovan*]. The most traditional military conflicts in the foreseeable future (up to 15 years [2030]) in the Central Asian and southwest strategic directions, as well as with internal military conflicts out to 30 years [2045], will be fought with conventional military actions at a scale of no more than local war. Over the [respective periods], the likely enemy or source of military threat in the western and eastern strategic directions, as well as in the Arctic region, will be capable of conducting high-tech military actions, where combined arms force groupings are essentially large combat supersystems that are able to react to changes in the operational situation in real time and preempt the enemy in employing fires, radioelectronic assets, and other forms of destructive means.

The most dangerous trend in the strategic nature of military dangers and threats is the appearance and buildup among probable enemies of the capabilities to neutralize the role of nuclear weapons as a factor of strategic deterrence. This capability will be achieved in the event that the United States and NATO countries are able to realize their plans in missile defense: the "Prompt Global Strike" concept, with the addition of conventional hypersonic missiles and future effective cyber weapons that are capable of disorganizing Russian communication systems and the combat C2 of Russia's strategic nuclear deterrence forces.

It is possible that the primary feature of military actions in all strategic directions 30 to 50 years from now will involve the employment of high-tech means of armed conflict in combination with intensive information-psychological actions in conditions in which the significance of the factor of strategic nuclear deterrence has significantly diminished.

CHAPTER SIX

The Assessment of the Condition of Russian National and Military Security: Established Process and Possible Paths to Improvement

Main Operations Directorate of the General Staff
Armed Forces of the Russian Federation
119160, Moscow, Frunzenskaia, 22/2

Summary

The article analyzes the established process for assessing Russian national and military security and describes possible ways to improve it. It examines deficiencies in the aggregate assessment indicators, which are legally regulated and currently in use. As a basis for identifying methods to fix the present flaws, we suggest the methodological tool developed by the 46th TsNII MOD for assessing military security; [this tool] ties together independent methods, models, and calculations. [The tool] analyzes the results obtained by [the independent methods] and presents generalized assessments of the functioning and development of the military organization of the Russian Federation. This article considers the methods proposed by the developers of this methodological tool for solving both *direct calculations* (the assessment of the level of military security of Russia, which can be assured under forecasted conditions using specific parameters of the structure of the military organization of the state) and *reciprocal calculations* (the task of finding the required level of military security and the justification of the structure of the military organization of the state, which in forecasted conditions and given present or future resources could ensure the military security of Russia). We conclude that future improvement of the method for assessing military security as a component of national security involves the formulation and selection of the rational courses of action to ensure Russia's military security on the basis of conditional indicators. The elements for solving this task could be the development of a mathematical model of a problematic situation and the associated decision, as well as the formalization of the required level of military security by using a tool based on the fuzzy sets theory. [This summary was included with the original article; it is not an addition by the editor.[1]]

The development of methods for the assessment of Russian military security is, at the present time, one of the most critical military-scientific tasks. The resolution of this task requires the search for and justification of rational ways to mitigate existing and forecasted military threats as well as to establish the [proper] force structure and training of the Armed Forces and other force components of the military organization of Russia.

Because the measures for ensuring military security are an integral part of a system of measures that ensure Russia's national security, the task of assessing both components is solved comprehensively. The National Security Strategy of the Russian Federation, which was confirmed by the Presidential Decree No. 683 on December 31, 2015 (hereafter, NSS),[2] dictates that control over the execution of the NSS is carried out within the framework of state monitoring of the condition of national security. The results of the monitoring are presented in the annual report of the Secretary of the Russian Security Council

---

[1] [Belokon', 2018.]

[2] President of the Russian Federation, "Decree of the President of the Russian Federation from 31.12.2015, On the National Security Strategy of the Russian Federation," No. 683, December 31, 2015.

to the president on the condition of national security and measures to strengthen it.[3]

The Statute on the Assessment and State Monitoring of the Condition of National Security of the Russian Federation (hereafter, Statute on the Assessment of National Security)[4] regulates the corresponding assessment process, which is understood as the analysis of the performance of execution of said documents and the determination of the level of accomplishment of objectives and tasks that are stipulated in strategic planning documents related to national security.

To conduct this assessment, constant monitoring takes place that includes the collection, processing, and analysis of information on the condition of national security; the forecast and identification of threats; and the formulation of options for command decisions on overcoming negative trends and crisis situations.

Monitoring the condition of national security is a practical mechanism for assessing the level of assurance of national interests and the achievement of strategic national priorities that are annotated in the NSS.

The primary tools for this assessment are indicators of the condition of Russian national security (hereafter, NS indicators), which are generalized characteristics that reflect the state of play in various areas relating to the assurance of national security (or the realization of strategic national priorities).

The aforementioned indicators are listed in the NSS and in the Statute on the Assessment of National Security.

In the NSS, there are ten primary NS indicators:

- the satisfaction of citizens with the level of protection of their constitutional rights and freedoms [and] their personal and property interests, including the protection from criminal actions

---

[3]   See Security Council of the Russian Federation, Statute No. 590, confirmed by Decree of the President of the Russian Federation on May 6, 2011.

[4]   The Office of the Security Council of the Russian Federation prepared a draft statute (Security Council of Russia, "On the Assessment and State Monitoring of the Condition of National Security of the Russian Federation," October 19, 2015).

- the share of modern weapons and military and special equipment in the Armed Forces of the Russian Federation, other forces [i.e., National Guard], combat formations, and [command] organs
- life expectancy
- gross domestic product (GDP) per capita
- decile coefficient (the ratio of the incomes of the top 10 percent of wealthiest and the incomes of the bottom 10 percent)
- level of inflation
- level of unemployment
- share of expenditures as a percent of GDP on science, technology, and education
- share of expenditures as a percent of GDP on culture
- share of Russian territory that is noncompliant with ecological regulations.[5]

In the Statute on the Assessment of National Security, there is an entire collection of national security indicators. More than 60 criteria, which were confirmed based on the recommendations of ministries and agencies as well as the scientific council of the Russian Security Council, are considered in the course of monitoring.[6]

The collection of indicators that was introduced in the Statute on the Assessment of National Security is used for the analysis of the level of execution of strategic national priorities that are established in the NSS: "defense of the country;" "state and social security;" "increase in quality of life of citizens;" "economic growth;" "science, technology, and education;" "health;" "culture;" "ecology of living systems and rational nature management;" "strategic stability and equal strategic partnership."

Analysis of all of the legislatively mandated mechanisms for the assessment of Russian national security has shown that the aforementioned 10 indicators, established by the NSS, are included in the aggregate criteria that are found within the Statute on the Assessment of National Security, but as "generic" independent indicators rather than primary indicators. At the same time, the concept of the "primary

---

5   President of the Russian Federation, 2015.

6   Security Council of the Russian Federation, 2015.

assessment indicator of the condition of Russian national security" is not defined in the NSS and is absent from the Statute.

A look into the connection between the primary indicators established in the NSS and the strategic national priorities does offer an answer to the question on the reasons for describing a number of characteristics of national security as primary. Of the ten strategic national priorities, the primary indicators of NS are distributed rather unevenly: four priorities have one primary indicator, one priority has two, and one has three primary indicators. Three strategic national priorities (science, technology, and education; health; strategic stability and equal strategic partnership) do not have primary indicators of NS.

The described inconsistency between the NSS and the Statute on the Assessment of National Security in terms of the indicators and their description as primary introduces into the assessment process a certain ambiguity. In this situation, it is necessary to take into account the sequence of passing the regulatory acts and the conduct of the assessment of national security and to use not the primary national security indicators in the NSS but the aggregate of characteristics that are provided in the Statute on the Assessment of National Security.

Analysis of the current process and aggregate indicators for assessing the condition of Russian national security highlights certain flaws.

First, the current process (which is described in open sources) does not consider the possibility of obtaining a generalized assessment of the condition of national security.

The advantage of introducing a generalized (aggregated) indicator of national security is based on the necessity of aligning the assessment criteria with overall requirements that are tied to assessment indicators (*Reliability and Effectiveness in Equipment*, 1988). One of the most important elements is correspondence with an objective, through which one can form a judgment in some situation on the level of achievement.

In this case, the objective is the assurance of Russian national security. The indicators of national security as generalized characteristics reflecting the condition of separate strategic national priorities cannot show the level of achievement of the stated task.

Therefore, if the generalized (aggregated) indicator is absent, then it is necessary to assess national security on the basis of more than 60 indicators within ten categories. However, in this case, a straightforward resolution of the assessment task becomes problematic when the values of one or several independent indicators go beyond acceptable norms.

Second, the indicators of national security do not directly assess the condition of the protection of individuals, society, and the state from internal and external threats (the definition [of NS] established in the National Security Strategy), which is Russian national security. The indicators are intended for the determination of the level of execution of objectives and tasks that are assigned in strategic planning documents in the sphere of national security as well as for analysis of the realization of plans in the documents. In other words, the assessment of the condition of protection of individuals, society, and the state from internal and external threats does not occur directly but indirectly through the results of actions taken to execute [the tasks] in the strategic planning documents. Such a process ties additional requirements to these documents, the goals and objectives of which together should adequately describe the condition of national security of the Russian Federation.

Third, the NS indicators are not categorized based on type of security, but rather on strategic national priorities, which does not allow for a determination of the degree to which the aggregate of these indicators captures the entire sphere of national security or characterize its condition.

Strategic national priorities are the most important areas in the assurance of national security. National security is assured through political, military, organizational, socio-economic, information, and legal actions of the executive entities, local authorities, and civil institutions directed at countering national security threats and pursuing national interests.[7] Thus, strategic national priorities are subprocesses of a single process [:] the functioning of the system for assuring national security. Evaluating this process within the bounds of each priority area and the results, it is possible to determine how effective the actions of executive entities and local authorities were. However,

---

7   President of the Russian Federation, 2015.

the question of how to correlate the obtained assessments with the condition of national security remains unclear.

Fourth, a conceptual tool is used in normative legal documents that limits the possibility of examining military security as a separate type of national security, which complicates coming up with a scientific-methodological tool for assessing Russian military security.

In accordance with the National Security Strategy, "national security includes the defense of the country and all other types of security that are noted in the Russian Constitution and legislation, particularly state, social, information, ecological, economic, transportation, and energy security and security of the individual."[8] Defense in this context is understood as a system of political, economic, military, social, legal, and other measures to prepare for the armed defense of the Russian Federation [and] the integrity and inviolability of its territory.[9] In other words, *national security* (as a condition of protection of the individual, society, and state from various threats) includes defense (as a system of measures), which is not entirely correct from the perspective of the systems approach.

It would be more effective, in our view, to consider and decompose national security into various types that were distinguished by the content and domain of the threat. Relatedly, many of the types of security that should be included are not only those that are found in the Constitution and legislation of the country, but the entire spectrum of existing and forecasted threats to the individual, society, and state.

Such an approach would offer the ability to assess the condition of national security based on indicators of the most important types [of security]: military, state, social, economic, information, etc.

***

The National Security Strategy and Military Doctrine of the Russian Federation generally determine the existing and future threats

---

[8]   President of the Russian Federation, 2015.

[9]   Government of the Russian Federation, Federal Law No. 61-FZ, "On Defense," May 31, 1996.

to national security and the areas of state activity to mitigate them.[10] "Russian national security" and "Russian military security," the interconnection of which is legally binding, is presented. . . .

Notably, the concept of Russian military security at the present time is not used in legislation and is only found in subordinate acts, such as in Presidential Decree No. 683, "On the National Security Strategy of the Russian Federation," from December 31, 2015, as well as in other decrees regulating the Russian military planning process. In accordance with the Military Doctrine of the Russian Federation, which introduces [the] term *military security*, [it] is defined as "the condition of protection of vitally important interests of the individual, society, and the state from external and internal military threats that are related to the use of military force or the threat of its use[; military security] is characterized by the absence of a military threat or the ability to counter the military threat." [11] In the assurance of national security, the protected objects are the individual, society, and the state.[12]

The primary obstacle that complicates the possibility of legislatively establishing the concept of military security is the separate use of the terms *defense* and *security* in the Russian constitution. This [document] serves as the basis for legal departments to forbid the "merging" in legislation of such concepts and, as a result, the inclusion of military security as one of the types of national security.

As a result, to resolve the task of systematic assessment of the condition of Russian national and military security, it is prudent to begin not from a legal perspective, but from a practical-logical and scientific-methodological perspective.

---

[10] Government of the Russian Federation, "Military Doctrine of the Russian Federation," December 30, 2014.

[11] The concept of *vitally important interests* was first used in Article 1 of the Law of the Russian Federation, "On Security," in 1992, and it was defined as "the aggregate of requirements, the satisfaction of which reliably ensures the existence and capabilities of the progressive development of the individual, society, and the state" (Government of the Russian Federation, Law No. 2446-I, "On Security," March 5, 1992).

[12] Government of the Russian Federation, 2014.

Figure 6.1
Connection Between the Concepts of Russian National Security and
Russian Military Security

National Security – the condition of protection of the individual, society, and the state from internal and external threats, through which are protected the realization of constitutional rights and freedoms of Russian citizens, a dignified quality and standard of living, sovereignty, independence, state and territorial integrity, and the stable socio-economic development of the Russian Federation.	Military Security – the condition of protection of vitally important interests of the individual, society, and the state from external and internal military threats that are related to the use of military force or the threat of its use[; military security] is characterized by the absence of a military threat or the ability to counter the military threat.

Protected object

Individual, society, state	Vitally important interests of the individual, society, and the state

Protecting entity

The state	The military organization of Russia

Sources of possible damage

Internal and external threats	External and internal military threats that are related to the use of military force or the threat of its use

Methods of protection

Political, economic, social, military, etc.	Military (related to the use of military force or threatened use of military force)

Thus, the assessment indicator for the condition of military security W_{MS} should be considered as one of the integral parts of the assessment indicator of national security WN_S.

As a specific form of a generalized indicator for the assessment of national security $W_{NS} = F(W_k)$ can be an additive or multiplicative convolution of independent assessment indicators of the condition of specific types of security W_k.

Such an approach would facilitate monitoring of the condition of national security based on the indicators of types of security, taking into account [the indicators'] importance for the assurance of national security in accordance with the planning period.

The calculation of the indicators that are most important for national security, including military, can be done on the basis of parameters of their condition P_k, which would be determined through monitoring. The methods of this calculation should be developed by the relevant specialized federal executive agencies of the Russian Federation. In addition, prior to presenting the aforementioned methods to the Secretary of the Security Council for approval, the methods must be considered during the meetings of the scientific council of the Russian Security Council.

C_c [is] criteria for assessing national security and a specific type of security, respectively; W_{NS} and W_{NS}^R [are] the value and required value, respectively, of the assessment indicator of national security; W_k and W_k^R [are] the value and required value, respectively, of an independent indicator for assessing a type of national security; and P_k and P_{MS} are the parameters of the condition of the type of national security and military security, respectively.

To apply the criteria K_{NS} and K_k . . . it is necessary to know the required values of national security, W_{NS}^R, and the specific types of national security, W_k^R.

Finding these values is a rather complex task. For example, the required value of military security depends not only on the characteristics of the force components of the Russian military organization but also on the parameters of the development of the VPO, the military and economic potentials of Russia's enemies and allies, and many other factors, including those that are of a subjective nature. The required

Figure 6.2
Relationship of Criteria and Indicators for Assessing the Condition of National and Military Security of the Russian Federation

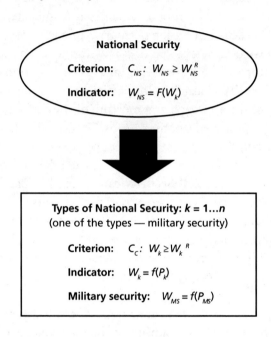

value of military security for the military organization may be determined (for example, through expert elicitation) to be such under certain military-political conditions, although the required value of military security for the same military organization could change by a wide margin in other conditions. In the most general sense, the considered correlation can be described in the following way: the higher the level of military security, the better (more effective) the employed measures in the sphere of defense.

To obtain quantitative assessments, it is necessary to formalize the required level of military security, which is tied to the diversity of components in the Russian military organization and the foreign and domestic conditions in which it functions; that is, to overcome the fixed uncertainty in accomplishing the task. Typically, this type of task is solved by using the fuzzy sets theory.[13]

The application of the aforementioned approach allows for the formulation and calculation of a generalized (aggregated) indicator of the condition of Russian national security in the end. It is sensible to delegate the task of development of this assessment tool, which is based on the indicators of the most important types of national security, to the Russian Security Council (with participation of the scientific council) and present the approach at a meeting of the Security Council.

Thus, the proposed approach provides generalized indicators for assessing the condition of national security. Relatedly, the indicators of national security that are established in the NSS and the Statute on the Assessment of National Security can be used as parameters of the condition of the respective types of national security.

It is worth noting that obtaining the assessments of the condition of national and military security is not an end in itself but a necessary part of planning and organizing counteraction to threats to the individual, society, and state, as well as military threats.

***

At the present time, there are a number of models and approaches to examine the level of functioning of the components of the Russian military organization. With respect to the military organization of the state, these models and approaches, as a rule, are loosely connected, independent methods—automated systems that have limited application.

As opposed to the aforementioned approach, a unique instrument that ties together the independent models and approaches and provides quantitative assessments of the measures for the assurance of military security within the bounds of the functional processes of the Russian military organization is that which was developed on the basis of a scientific-methodological tool for the assessment of military security at the 46th TsNII MOD.[14] This assessment tool establishes the sequence

[13] D. A. Pospelov, ed., *Fuzzy Sets in Command and Control and Artificial Intelligence Models*, Nauka, 1986; and S. P. Belokon', "Fuzzy Methods for Assessing Military Command and Control Systems," *Bulletin of the Academy of Military Sciences*, Vol. 4, No. 9, 2004.

[14] Tsyrendorzhiev, 2014.

for using the aggregate of the methods, models, and calculation tasks to assess the results obtained from the independent methods and to calculate generalized assessments of the functioning and development of the Russian military organization. The use of this tool provides the possibility for parametric combination of individual methods, and, in the future, [the possibility] to apply these methods to military planning by detailing the respective subject areas.

The presence of such a tool lends the aggregate of existing methods and models used for military planning a new quality that facilitates the resolution of both "direct" and "reciprocal" calculation tasks. . . .

A direct calculation task is included in

- the forecast of military-political, strategic, economic, scientific-technical, technological, demographic, and other conditions, in which in the long-term perspective Russian military security must be ensured;
- the justification of the parameters of the structure of the military organization of the state in forecasted conditions.

In the resolution of direct calculation tasks, the aforementioned scientific-methodological tool assists in the assessment of the level of Russian military security, which can be maintained in forecasted conditions given specific parameters of the military organization of the state. This allows for a comparison of various options for the [structure of] the latter, and [allows decisionmakers] to choose the most rational of them.

The reciprocal task includes setting the required level of military security and the justification of the structure of the military organization of the state, which in forecasted conditions, given existing or expected resource capabilities, could ensure Russian military security. The resolution of this task produces additional requirements, [both] for the aggregate of methods, models, and calculation tasks of military planning and for its constituent, individual methods.

The sequence of the application of the military security assessment tool in solving the reciprocal calculation task of justifying the

Figure 6.3
Consolidated Algorithm for the Application of a Scientific-Methodological Assessment of Military Security in the Resolution of Direct and Reciprocal Calculation Tasks

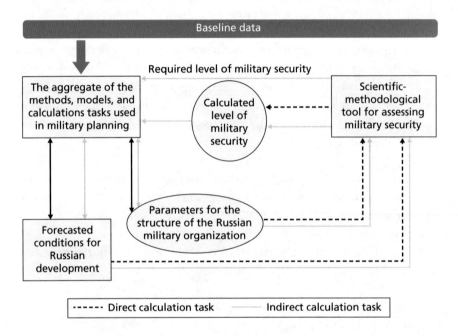

rational options for the force components of the Russian military organization to ensure the required level of military security is shown. . . .

To formalize the assessment, military security can be understood as a condition of interstate (military-political) relations and the defense capability of the state, by which the probability of military conflicts is reduced to a minimum[;] neither side has any incentive to initiate hostilities against the other and neither is put into conditions requiring urgent measures to prevent a disadvantageous situation.

This suggests a division of two groups of factors that influence the condition of military security:

- military-political relations
- defense capability of the state.

By employing such a methodological approach along with independent methods that are used in military planning, the interrelationships between the level of military security of the state, the situation in the foreign policy and military spheres, and the correlation of military and economic potentials of Russia and other actors are formalized.

The VPO in this case is understood as the result of the interaction of military-political actors conducting military policy in pursuit of their own national interests. It is proposed that the effect of this interaction at the level of military-political actors is demonstrated in the impact on a certain aggregate of factors that are considered in the determination of objectives and tasks of military policy and the forms and methods of their execution.

Economic and political interests determine the essence, content, and direction of Russian military policy as well as that of other military-political actors. Military policy must ensure favorable, mutually beneficial economic, political, cultural, scientific, and other ties and relations with all countries, especially neighboring countries. The

Figure 6.4
The Sequence of the Application of the Military Security Assessment Tool in Solving the Reciprocal Calculation Task of Justifying the Rational Options for the Force Components of the Russian Military Organization to Ensure the Required Level of Military Security

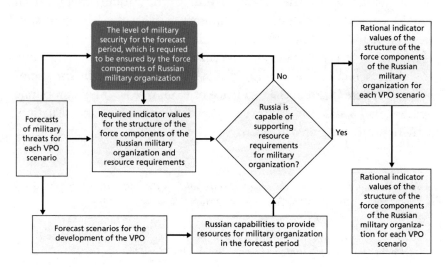

understanding of potential and existing capabilities of the state to pursue its interests plays a role in the formation of military policy.

Military policy as a part of foreign and domestic policy of VPO actors is demonstrated in various spheres of interaction between states and their coalitions. The primary areas of interaction include foreign policy, military, socio-political, and economic ([Voloshko and Lutovinov], 2007).[15] In several works,[16] information, religion, and territory are included [to these areas of state interaction].

Among the many parameters of military policy of other actors, of greatest interest are those by which it is possible to judge the degree of aggressiveness and hostility toward Russia. Such parameters are defined for the policy of an actor in the aforementioned four areas.

In the area of foreign policy, military policy parameters of VPO actors include: the domestic political situation in neighboring countries, the activity of states that increases tension in bilateral relations with Russia, the activity of other actors subject to international law that increase tension, international-legal aspects of interaction between Russia and other actors subject to international law, [and] the international-legal aspects of the interaction of Russia with other states.

The military policy parameters of an actor in the military sphere [include]: the activity of other countries in the information confrontation domain, actions taken by states and other actors under international law to prepare the theater of military operations, mobilization activities of states, the direction of military activity of other actors subject to international law, [and] the condition of troop (force) groupings of the armed forces of states and the emphasis in their combat training.

Parameters in the military policy of a VPO actor in the socio-political sphere include: the influence of foreign mass media on public opinion in Russia, the context of the development of the situation, activities of other states affecting the socio-political situation in third

---

[15] A. A. Prokhozhev, ed., *General Theory of National Security: Textbook*, Russian Academy of Public Administration, 2002; V. K. Senchagov, ed., *Economic Security of Russia: General Course: Textbook*, Delo, 2005.

[16] Markova Adler and Granovskii, 1976; and V. A. Polegaev, "Nonnuclear Strategic Deterrence. Myths and Reality," *Strategic Stability*, Vol. 1, No. 42, 2008.

countries in the context of their relations with Russia, actions conducted from abroad to exacerbate social and ethnic disputes in border areas of Russia, the condition of international public opinion in regard to policies of Russia and its allies, [and[the formation of public opinion in other states in regard to the policies of Russia and its allies.

The parameters of military policy in the economic sphere are: impact of global economic and financial actors on the state of the mobilization capabilities of the Russian economy using methods that are not sanctioned by international law, foreign economic relations of other states with other actors, the condition of Russia's economic relations with foreign states and other actors subject to international law, [and] financial-economic indicators of military preparations of other states.

The degree of hostility in the military policy in each of the parameters can vary.

The military security assessment method proposes indicators of hostility in various parameters of military policy of a VPO actor and defines possible qualitative values of these indicators that could be achieved depending on the obtained (forecasted) results of the execution of policy.[17]

Parameter indicators of military policy are understood as qualitative results in each of the [four] aforementioned areas. For example, the condition of military infrastructure assets, the system of state and military C2, the effectiveness of the training of military-ready reserve, the condition of the armed forces of the state, the level of hostility in their combat training can all be considered indicator results.

The value of each of these indicators can vary depending on the military-political objective that is being pursued by a VPO actor as well as on the time and resources that are committed to achieving it as of the time of the assessments. Relatedly, the VPO assessment should be conducted at several points in time as events occur in relations between Russia and specific actors. This offers the possibility to assess the trends and future development of the situation and the direction of military policy.

---

[17] Tsyrendorzhiev, 2014.

[Figure] shows a functional architecture of the scientific-methodological tool for assessing the military security of the Russian Federation. It is based on expert-analytical methods for assessing the degree of hostility in military-political relations and for comparing the potential of the Russian Federation with the potentials of other military actors. Based on this framework, the level of military threats is determined and the ability to mitigate them through measures of strategic deterrence is analyzed. The residual potential of the military threat provides the conclusion on the level of Russian military security.

This application of the scientific-methodological tool for assessing military security is a direct calculation task. Its use in solving a reciprocal calculation task is done in the following way.

For the planning period, there is a required level of military security. A forecast is conducted using relevant methods for the following:

- scenarios of the development of the VPO and strategic situation [latter refers to strategic nuclear balance and actions affecting it]
- the possible character of military conflicts.

This helps to determine the levels of hostility and presumed potential of VPO actors. For each considered scenario, tasks and requirements are determined for the force components of the military organization of the state, variants of the necessary combat strength of the armed forces, other forces, combat formations and agencies for peacetime and wartime, and also requirements for their armament system and mobilization potential.

Next, there is a calculation for the resource requirements to build the necessary structure of the force components of the military organization of the state and a forecast of the economic capabilities of the state.

If the results are in accordance with the assigned tasks, the assessed option for developing the military organization of the state can be considered rational.

In the case in which the resource requirements are not compatible with existing economic capabilities, then the tasks and requirements for the military organization force components (on account of corrections to strategic deterrence policy and the employment of nonmilitary

Figure 6.5
Functional Architecture of the Scientific-Methodological Tool for Assessing the Military Security of the Russian Federation

measures to reduce the conflict potential in the VPO) or the requirements for the level of military security will be adjusted. Then the aforementioned procedures are repeated.

The military security assessment tool establishes baseline information for the aggregate of methods, models, and calculations used in military planning and allows for the practical use of the results obtained with them. This offers the possibility to justify the required correlation of force components of the Russian military organization and a possible enemy to ensure military security. The correlation of forces, obtained in this way, will correspond to the requirements of defense sufficiency and take into account the influence of strategic deterrence factors and the forecasted results of the employment of nonmilitary measures to mitigate military threats.

***

Thus, on the basis of the proposed approach to assessing the condition of national and military security, a universal scientific-methodological tool can be created to conduct comparative analysis of various options for measures in the area of defense and to ensure Russia's national security. However, the solution to this problem involves conducting special studies to form a set of baseline data; first of all, for the method assessing military security as well as to construct functions that describe the degree to which the actual results of the functioning of the military organization of the state meet required parameters. [These functions should also] formalize the requirements of the decisionmaker at various stages of choosing a rational option for ensuring Russian military security. Future improvement of the method for assessing military security, in our view, requires the determination of the options on the basis of the indicators of the condition of military security. An element of the method could be the construction of a mathematical model of the situation for decisionmaking that applies the concept of an operation as an aggregate of targeted actions for ensuring Russian military security that are united under a general plan of action and a single objective.[18] Such a model must, with some degree of detail, describe all of the primary processes for ensuring Russian military security; that is, it should be a model of the functioning of the military organization of the state. The construction of such a model is a large-scale and labor-intensive task because it requires the formalization of complex planning processes and the execution of a system of military and nonmilitary measures by leadership, force, and support components of Russia's military organization. The mechanism of these processes remains insufficiently studied.

Literature

1. Iu. P. Adler, E. V. Markova, and Iu. V. Granovskii, *Experiment Planning in the Search for Optimal Conditions*, Nauka, 1976.

2. S. P. Belokon', "Fuzzy Methods for Assessing Military Command and Control Systems," *Bulletin of the Academy of Military Sciences*, Vol. 4, No. 9, 2004.

---

[18] F. M. Morse and D. E. Kimball, *Operations Research Methods*, Sovetskoe radio, 1956; V. I. Serdiukov, *Primary Concepts in the Theory of Combat Effectiveness*, Moscow: Military Academy of Armored Forces, 1995, pp. 37–39; and V. N. Iurkov, ed., *Operations Research*, VIA, 1990.

3. V. S. Voloshko and V. I. Lutovinov, *Military Policy and Military Security of the Russian Federation in Conditions of Globalization*, A. S. Rukshin, ed., Center for Military-Strategic Studies of the General Staff of the Russian Armed Forces, 2007.

4. V. N. Iurkov, ed., *Operations Research*, VIA, 1990, pp. 25–28.

5. F. M. Morse and D. E. Kimball, *Operations Research Methods*. Sovetskoe radio, 1956, pp. 37–39.

6. V. F. Utkin and Iu. V. Kriuchkov, eds., *Reliability and Effectiveness in Equipment*, Vol. 3, *Effectiveness of Technical Systems*, 1988.

7. D. A. Pospelov, ed., *Fuzzy Sets in Command and Control and Artificial Intelligence Models*, Nauka, 1986.

8. A. A. Prokhozhev, ed., *General Theory of National Security: Textbook*, Russian Academy of Public Administration, 2002.

9. V. I. Polegaev, "Nonnuclear Strategic Deterrence: Myths and Reality," *Strategic Stability*, Vol. 1, No. 42, 2008.

10. V. I. Serdiukov, *Primary Concepts in the Theory of Combat Effectiveness*, Military Academy of Armored Forces, 1995.

11. S. R. Tsyrendorzhiev, "On the Quantitative Assessment of the Degree of Military Security," *Military Thought*, No. 10, 2014, pp. 27–40.

12. V. K. Senchagov, ed., *Economic Security of Russia: General Course: Textbook*, Delo, 2005.

References

References below include citations from all sections of this volume, including the Introduction. Citations are reproduced here as found in the original articles with minor formatting changes.

Adler, Iu. P., E. V. Markova, and Iu. V. Granovskii, *Experiment Planning in the Search for Optimal Conditions*, Moscow: Nauka, 1976.

Annenkov, V. I., S. N. Baranov et al. *Security of Russia: Geopolitical and Military-Political Aspects*, RUSAVIA, 2006.

Barynkin, V. M., "Otsenka voenno-politicheskoi obstanovki: metodologicheskii aspekt," *Voennaia mysl'*, No. 5, 1999, pp. 23–30.

Belokon', S. P., "Fuzzy Methods for Assessing Military Command and Control Systems," *Bulletin of the Academy of Military Sciences*, Vol. 4, No. 9, 2004.

Belokon', S. P., "Otsenivanie sostoianiia natsional'noi i voennoi bezopasnosti Rossii: ustanovlennyi poriadok i vozmozhnye puti sovershenstvovaniia [The Assessment of the Condition of Russian National and Military Security: Established Process and Possible Paths to Improvement]," *Vestnik Moskovskogo gosudarstvennogo universiteta, Seriia 25, Mezhdunarodnye otnosheniia i mirovaia politika*, Vol. 1, 2018, pp. 20–41.

Burenok, V. M., ed., *Kontseptsiia obosnovaniia perspektivnogo oblika silovykh komponentov voennoi organizatsii Rossiiskoi Federatsii*, Izdatel'skii dom Granitsa, 2018.

Chuev, Yu. V., and Yu. B. Mikhailov, *Prognozirovanie v voennom dele [Forecasting in Military Affairs: A Soviet View]*, trans. DGIS Multilingual Section, Translation Bureau, Secretary of State Department, Ottawa, Canada, Washington, D.C.: Department of the Air Force, February 6, 1981.

Derbin, E. A., and A. I. Podberezkin, "Perspektivnyi oblik voennoi organizatsii Rossiskoi Federatsii," *Vestnik MGIMO Universiteta*, Vol. 3, No. 30, 2018, pp. 210–224.

Dynkin, A. A., ed., *Mir 2035. Global'nyi prognoz*, Magistr, 2017.

Gerasimov, V. V., "Rol' General'nogo shtabe v organizatsii oborony strany v sootvetstvii s novym polozheniem o General'nom shtabe, utverzhdennym prezidenta Rossiiskoi Federatsii," *Vestnik Akademii voennykh nauk*, Vol. 1, No. 46, 2014, pp. 14–22.

Gerasimov, V. V., "Opyt strategicheskogo rukovodstva v Velikoi otechestvennoi voyni i organizatsiia edinogo upravleniia oboronoi strany v sovremennykh usloviiakh," *Vestnik Akademii voennykh nauk*, Vol. 2, No. 51, 2015.

Government of the Russian Federation, Law No. 2446-I, "On Security," March 5, 1992.

Government of the Russian Federation, Federal Law No. 61-FZ, "On Defense," May 31, 1996.

Government of the Russian Federation, "Military Doctrine of the Russian Federation," February 5, 2010.

Government of the Russian Federation, "Military Doctrine of the Russian Federation," December 30, 2014.

Iurkov, V. N., ed., *Operations Research*, VIA, 1990.

Library of Congress of the United States, "Russian Romanization Table," webpage, undated. As of December 4, 2020: https://www.loc.gov/catdir/cpso/romanization/russian.pdf

Mattis, Jim, *Summary of the 2018 National Defense Strategy of the United States of America: Sharpening the American Military's Competitive Edge*, Washington, D.C.: U.S. Department of Defense, 2018.

Morse, F. M., and D. E. Kimball, *Operations Research Methods*, Sovetskoe radio, 1956.

Mukhin, Vladimir, "Moskva korektiruet Voennuyu doktrinu," *Nezavisimaya gazeta*, August 1, 2014.

Podberezkin, A. I., ed., *Strategicheskoe prognozirovanie i planirovanie vneshei i oboronnoi politiki*, Moscow: MGIMO University Press, Vol. 1, 2015.

Polegaev, V. I., "Nonnuclear Strategic Deterrence. Myths and Reality," *Strategic Stability*, Vol. 1, No. 42, 2008, pp. 64–67.

Popov, I. M., and M. M. Khamzatov, *Voina budushchego*, 3rd ed., Moscow: Kuchkovo pole, 2018.

Pospelov, D. A., ed., *Fuzzy Sets in Command and Control and Artificial Intelligence Models*, Moscow: Nauka, 1986.

Pozdniakov, Aleksandr, "Metodologiia otsenki voenno-politicheskoi obstanovki v interesakh obespecheniia gosudarstvennoi bezopasnosti Rossiiskoi Federatsii," lecture for the FSB, undated.

President of the Russian Federation, "Decree of the President of the Russian Federation from 31.12.2015, On the National Security Strategy of the Russian Federation," No. 683, December 31, 2015.

Prokhozhev, A. A., ed., *General Theory of National Security: Textbook*, Russian Academy of Public Administration, 2002.

Reach, Clint, Alyssa Demus, Eugeniu Han, Bilyana Lilly, Krystyna Marcinek, and Yuliya Shokh, *Russian Military Forecasting and Analysis: The Military-Political Situation and Military Potential in Strategic Planning*, Santa Monica, Calif.: RAND Corporation, forthcoming.

Rogozin, D. O., ed., *War and Peace in Terms and Definitions*, Moscow: Veche, 2004.

Russian Academy of Missile and Artillery Sciences, *Works of the All-Russia Scientific-Practical Conference on "Current Problems in Defense and Security,"* Vol. 3: *Arms and Military Equipment*, St. Petersburg, 2015.

Security Council of the Russian Federation, Statute No. 590, confirmed by Decree of the President of the Russian Federation on May 6, 2011.

Security Council of Russia, "On the Assessment and State Monitoring of the Condition of National Security of the Russian Federation," October 19, 2015.

Senchagov, V. K., ed., *Economic Security of Russia: General Course: Textbook*, Moscow: Delo, 2005.

Serdiukov, V. I., *Primary Concepts in the Theory of Combat Effectiveness*, Moscow: Military Academy of Armored Forces, 1995.

Tsyrendorzhiev, Sambu, "Prognoz voennykh opasnostei i ugroz Rossii," *Zashchita i bezopasnost'*, Vol. 4, 2015, pp. 10–14.

Tsyrendorzhiev, S. R., "O kolichestvennoi otsenke stepeni voennoi bezopasnosti [On the Quantitative Assessment of the Degree of Military Security]," *Voennaia mysl'*, No. 10, 2014, pp. 27–40.

Utkin, V. F., and Iu. V. Kriuchkov, eds., *Reliability and Effectiveness in Equipment*, Vol. 3: *Effectiveness of Technical Systems*, 1988.

Voloshko, V. S., and V. I. Lutovinov, *Voennaia politika i voennaia bezopasnost' Rossiiskoi Federatsii v usloviiakh globalizatsii*, Moscow: Voennoe izdatel'stvo, 2007.